HORSES AND PONIES

KT-362-992

A KINGFISHER BOOK
First published in Great Britain in 1979
by Ward Lock Limited, 116 Baker Street, London, W1M 2BB,
a member of the Pentos Group.

Designed and produced by Grisewood & Dempsey Ltd
Grosvenor House, 141-143 Drury Lane, London WC2
© Grisewood & Dempsey Ltd 1979

Colour separations by Newsele Litho Ltd, Milan, London
Printed and bound by Vallardi Industrie Grafiche, Milan

BRITISH LIBRARY CATALOGUING IN PUBLICATION DATA
Henschel, Georgie
  Horses and ponies. – (Kingfisher guides).
  1. Horses – Juvenile literature   2. Ponies –
  Juvenile literature
  I. Title   II. Inglefield, Eric   III. Series
  636.1   SF302

  ISBN 0-7063-5849-X

AUTHOR
GEORGIE HENSCHEL

EDITOR
ERIC INGLEFIELD

CONSULTANT
ROBERT OWEN

CONTENTS

INTRODUCTION

All horses and ponies have the same bone structure; they are all variations of the same basic pattern. All, therefore, have the same *points*, the term used to describe the parts of a horse's body, although each breed will have its own characteristics. Animals bred for particular purposes will have particular points differently developed. A horse can have good, and bad, points. A well-made horse or pony of any breed will have the good points of that breed, and will give the appearance of being balanced and in proportion. The Shire and the Thoroughbred, for example, are horses totally different in type, since one is bred for extreme strength and pulling power, the other for extreme speed. Although they have the same points, the sum of those points, or their *conformation*, is quite different. Yet each, being good of its own breed, is in proportion and pleasing to look at.

Horses are equines over 14.2 hands (hh) in height, a hand being 4 inches (10 cm). There are three types: *hot bloods*, such as the Arabian and the Thoroughbred, which for centuries have been among mankind's most prized possessions; *cold bloods*, which, as the work-horses of the world, have pulled man's loads, tilled his land and helped him to prosperity; and *warm bloods*, which are a mixture of the two, and include the majority of today's riding and driving horses, hunters, show-jumpers and eventers.

Ponies are equines under 14.2 hh in height. But it is not only height that distinguishes them. Descended mostly from the primitive Celtic Pony or Forest Horse, or from a mixture of the two, and accustomed for far longer than any breed of horse to living free and fending for themselves, they have developed differently. Ponies are shorter in the leg than horses, the cannon bone, in particular, being shorter. Because they are therefore stockier than horses, ponies are often capable of carrying considerable weight in proportion to their size. Their heads vary in

A horse bred for speed.

A horse bred for strength.

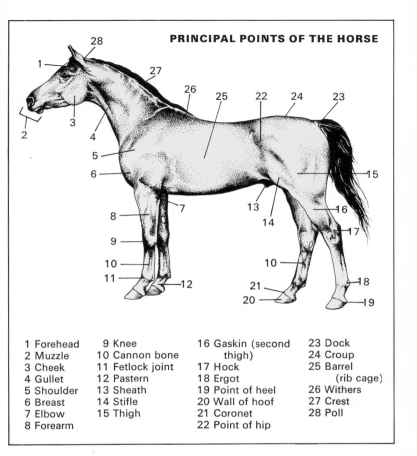

PRINCIPAL POINTS OF THE HORSE

1 Forehead	9 Knee	16 Gaskin (second thigh)	23 Dock
2 Muzzle	10 Cannon bone	17 Hock	24 Croup
3 Cheek	11 Fetlock joint	18 Ergot	25 Barrel
4 Gullet	12 Pastern	19 Point of heel	(rib cage)
5 Shoulder	13 Sheath	20 Wall of hoof	26 Withers
6 Breast	14 Stifle	21 Coronet	27 Crest
7 Elbow	15 Thigh	22 Point of hip	28 Poll
8 Forearm			

width, but are never long, heavy or Roman-nosed; their ears are neat and small and their outlook alert, as though they were always taking stock of their surroundings. They grow long protective coats in winter, and long mane and tail hair to ward off winter cold and summer flies. They have good hard feet, are sure-footed, and have a highly developed instinct for finding their way safely across country and through water.

Ponies also differ from horses in character. The Arab apart, they probably have more innate intelligence than the average horse (unkind people call it cunning) and more self-reliance. They have owed little to mankind through the ages. Although they appreciate being well looked after and will serve willingly in return, they always maintain that sturdy independence of spirit which has enabled them to survive long periods of human neglect.

Bay (*with black mane, tail and legs*)

Chestnut

Brown

Black

Colours

The principal true colours of horses are bay, brown, chestnut and black and, for many native or ancient breeds, dun. There are also many grey horses, but grey, like many mixed coat colours, is in fact the result of pigmentation failure, or variation. A grey horse must have had one grey parent, and all greys grow lighter with age, ending up white. Foals seldom keep the colour with which they are born, their adult colour usually establishing itself when they are about two years old. The colour of their muzzles and of the hair around their eyes will often reveal what that colour will be.

A bay horse always has a black mane and tail, and black legs, usually from the knees and hocks downwards. A brown horse may have much the same body colour as a bay, but it will have a brown mane and tail and brown legs. There are many shades of chestnut, from *liver*, really more the colour of milk chocolate, to pale gold; chestnuts are always

Grey

Dun (*here a yellow dun*)

Roan (*here a strawberry roan*)

Piebald (*behind*) *and skewbald*

wholly chestnut, with no black. True black is rare; a black horse will have a black muzzle, but if the muzzle shows brown, the horse is dark brown. Dun horses carry an eel stripe and some have zebra markings on the legs. There are many shades of dun. Grey duns can go white with age, and the eel stripe will fade. Pale yellow duns, golden duns and mouse duns have dark manes and do not change with age. The coats of roan horses are flecked through with white hairs. There are three shades of roan: strawberry, bay and blue. Piebald horses are black and white, while skewbald horses are brown and white, or brown and black, or any other colour and white. The Palomino colour is truly golden, the mane and tail silvery, not just paler. The only truly white horse is an albino, which has a pink, not a grey, skin, and usually pale blue eyes.

Most of the names of coat colours are in world-wide use, but some countries have special ones of their own. In America, for example, a rich, reddish-coloured chestnut is called a *sorrel*.

Star

Stripe

**Wall
eye**

Markings

Most horses have white markings, apart from some of the native pony breeds, which should not have any. Horses and ponies registered in the Stud Books of their breed must have their markings clearly described. Racehorses today travel about with passports, like humans. Markings are those seen on the head and legs. A small white patch anywhere on the body – sometimes due to an injury – must also be described, but is called simply a *patch*.

The names of the markings are logical, although a white one in the centre of the forehead is always called a *star*, even if it is not exactly star-shaped. A white line running down the face is a *stripe*. Many horses have both, which is called a *star and stripe*. A broad white band running down the centre of the face, often widening towards the muzzle, is a *blaze*. If the white extends beyond the front of the face, and around the eyes, it is a *white face*. A small white mark between or on the nostrils, is a *snip*. Some horses,

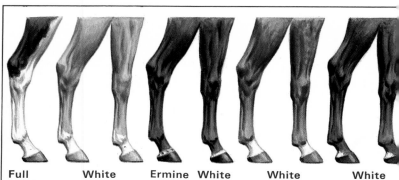

| Full stocking | White fetlocks | Ermine | White coronet | White pasterns | White heels |

Blaze

Snip

...ite face ...th flesh ...rk

particularly chestnuts, have hairless pink patches round the mouth and muzzle; these are *flesh marks*. A *wall-eye* is an eye with a very pale blue, almost white, iris.

Names of the leg markings are equally logical. White extending right up the leg, usually on the inside, to the thigh or elbow is a *full stocking;* up to the knee or hock, a *stocking;* half way up, a *sock*. If the white covers the fetlock joint, it is known as a *white fetlock*. If it stops short of the fetlock, it is a *white pastern*. A small band of white just above and around the top of the hoof is a *white coronet*. A white coronet is often flecked with black; this is called *ermine*, because it resembles the black flecking of ermine fur. An unusual marking is white at the back of the foot; this is a *white heel*.

The colour of the hoofs must also be described. Usually, the hoof of a leg with white markings will also be white, except for white coronets or heels, when the hoof is more generally black.

A luxuriant mane and forelock;
characteristic of pony breeds.

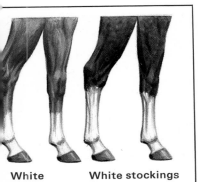

White socks   **White stockings**

Size and Age

In most English-speaking countries, horses are measured in hands (hh), a hand being four inches (10 cm). The measurement is taken from the ground to the highest point of the withers. While some breeds mature more quickly than others, a horse is not fully mature until it is five years old, when it is considered to have attained its full height. This is a point to remember. If horses or ponies are worked hard when too young, they are liable to develop unsoundness, particularly of the legs, and their working lives will be shortened. Also, because horses, like humans, develop mentally as well as physically, they can become sour and un-cooperative, simply through having been unable to understand what has been asked of them.

One year of a horse's life roughly corresponds to about 3½ of a human's, the major difference being that foals are born with the use of their legs and are able to keep up with their elders a few hours after birth. Probably for this reason people tend to think young horses more mature than they really are. When horses are very old, 20 and over, their backs tend to become dipped, they may have deep hollows above their eyes, and they may go grey about the face. Mares, however, never stop being able to breed, and stallions can remain potent all their lives.

Knowledgeable people tell a horse's age by its teeth. Horses have two kinds: *incisors* at the front for grazing, and *molars* at the back for grinding and chewing. Between the two is a convenient gap for the bit to lie in, called the *bars* of the mouth. Male horses also have *tushes*, two in the

A very old horse with a typically dipped back.

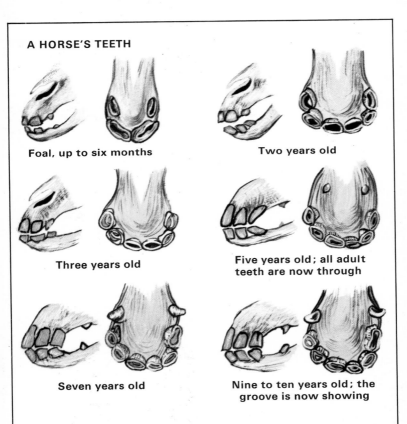

A HORSE'S TEETH

Foal, up to six months

Two years old

Three years old

Five years old; all adult teeth are now through

Seven years old

Nine to ten years old; the groove is now showing

upper jaw and two in the lower. Until horses are two years old, they have *milk*, or *baby*, teeth, which are gradually replaced by the permanent ones.

Both sets of teeth have three pairs of incisors. Foals are usually born with the central pair just through. By the age of two, they will have all three pairs, which then start to be replaced by the permanent ones. A pair appears each year, the central pair first, so that by the time a horse is five, it will have all three pairs of its permanent incisors or a 'full mouth'. If a male, it will probably have its tushes. At ten, a groove appears at the top centres of the corner incisor, called *Galvayne's groove*, which gradually extends down the length of the tooth.

Horses' teeth continue to grow all through life. As their gums recede with age, old horses appear to have very long teeth, hence the expression 'long in the tooth'.

Stables and Grazing

To keep horses permanently stabled takes up a lot of time. Not only must they be regularly fed and their boxes kept clean, but every day, come rain or shine, they must be exercised. Stabled horses can be very keen rides; not all owner-riders are experienced enough to cope with them.

The most satisfactory way is to keep them on the 'combined system': in winter, in at night, and out by day when not being ridden; in summer, out at night, and in by day. When out, horses will give themselves some exercise and use up some of their surplus energy. Children's ponies are best kept this way in spring and summer. If they are out all the time when the grass is lush, they easily become too fat, and may develop laminitis, which is a painful fever of the foot.

Owners of horses or ponies should either possess or have the lease of a paddock, as all horses, even permanently stabled ones, benefit from a few hours' freedom now and then. Loose boxes need not be elaborate but they should be draughtproof and sited where they get some sun, and where the horses can see one another. A box for a single horse should preferably be sited near the house where the horse will have plenty to look at, and so not become bored. The doors should be in two halves. The top half should always be kept open, unless a blizzard or gale is blowing directly in; the bottom half should have two bolts. Mangers should be fitted in a corner, and each box should have a strong tie-ring. Hay can be fed in a net tied to the ring, or from a rack.

For horses, boxes should be not less than 12 feet by 10 (3½ metres by 3), while 10 feet by 10 (3 metres by 3) is sufficient for ponies.

All native ponies are healthier living out. Their field should have good fences or hedges, and the gate a secure fastener. Barbed wire should not be used. If there is no running water, the ponies will need a water trough; if no natural shelter, a three-sided field shelter will be appreciated. Grass needs to be kept in good condition. If the pony owner has only one field, it is best to divide it, grazing each part alternately and fertilising when necessary. In small fields, droppings should be picked up as often as possible or the ground will become 'horsesick' and a home for worm larvae, which will re-infect the animals as they graze. Animals living out must be visited and checked every day. They appreciate this and learn to look forward to the daily visit. Caring for horses or ponies, in or out, is a responsibility that must be accepted. The reward is to have friendly, contented animals in good condition.

Stable doors should be in two halves: the top one left open, the bottom one closed with two bolts.

Fields should be well fenced, with secure gates. Water should always be available, and shelter is advisable.

A stabled horse, bedded for the night, has its night rug on and its hay net neatly tied. The horse is tied while the droppings are removed.

Feeding

Horses grazing at liberty eat more or less constantly. They have relatively small stomachs, and their digestive systems are not geared to cope with large meals at fairly long intervals, as are our own. Horses and ponies that work need two kinds of food: *bulk*, which is grass or hay; and energy-producing food, or *concentrates*. The amount of concentrates any horse needs is governed by the horse's size and the work it is doing. Horses are individuals; there is no hard-and-fast rule that will apply to them all. A rough guide is that a 15 hh horse of average build will need a total of 25 lbs (11.34 kg) of food in 24 hours. Add or subtract 1 lb (0.45 kg) for every inch (25 mm) taller or smaller and the result will not be far wrong. The total is then divided into bulk and concentrates, the total weight of which should remain constant. To make up 25 lb (11.34 kg) of food, 9 lbs

(4 kg) of concentrates can be given with 16 lbs (7.25 kg) of hay; if more concentrates, less hay; if less concentrates, more hay. A horse which is laid off work for any reason must have its concentrate ration reduced at once.

Stabled horses should have their total concentrate ration divided into four feeds; combined system horses, into three; and ponies living out, into two: one when brought in before riding, the other on return. No single concentrate, or 'short' feed, should weigh more than 4 lbs (1.8 kg). The largest portion of the hay ration should be given at night. Horses should not be worked hard until an hour after a feed. If they have water always available, they will never drink too much. They should be wormed regularly, at least every three months, and have a salt or mineral lick in their box or field.

The principal energy foods, or concentrates, are: oats, various brands of cubes and flaked barley. Bran is good for the digestion; some can be added to each short feed and it is beneficial fed as a mash. Additional feeds are boiled whole barley and flaked maize, which are both good in winter; sugar-beet pulp or nuts, which are appetizing, but must be soaked; molasses and molassine meal, which are good for the digestion; and linseed, mash or gruel, which put a gloss on the coat. Sliced carrots should be fed as often as possible in winter. All animals wintering out should have as much hay as they will eat, and if the weather is hard, a short feed as well.

Grooming

Stabled horses and those kept on the combined system should be groomed thoroughly every day. This should take at least 45 minutes. Horses living out should not have too much natural grease taken out of their coats, but they must be kept clean, their legs free of mud, and their feet regularly picked out. After riding, the saddle patch and where the girth lies should be brushed before the horses are turned out.

Grooming Kit

Dandy brush

Body brush

Water brush

Metal curry comb

Mane comb

Rubber curry comb

Hoof pick

Stable rubber

Small sponges

When buying grooming kit, it is worth remembering that pure bristle, though expensive, is better than nylon for both dandy and body brushes. Nylon brushes, if used, should never be dried near heat, as they congeal.

Tack Cleaning Kit

Tin of oil

Sponge

Duster

Saddle soap

THE HORSE THROUGH HISTORY

Origins and Evolution

The ancestor of the horse was an animal called *Eohippus*, which was about the size of a fox, and had four pads instead of a hoof. It developed through several stages of evolution until by the time cave drawings and ancient records began to exist, it had become a recognisable horse, called *Equidae*. This is the general name for all members of the horse family, which includes the Ass and the Zebra. The horse itself is called *Equus Caballas;* the ass, *Equus Hemiones;* and the zebra, *Equus Zebra.*

Through time, the horse branch of the family began to develop into different types, according to the parts of the world and the climates into which it wandered. As Man himself developed differently according to where he lived, so did the horse, adapting in size, type and conformation to its environment. Horse and pony breeds as we know them today spring from four principal divisions of the horse family: the Oriental; the Mongolian; the North European and North Asian Forest Horse; and the Celtic, or Atlantic, pony.

A prehistoric cave painting

The Mongolian Wild Horse

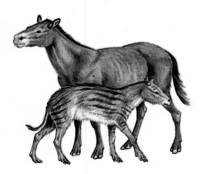

Paintings by prehistoric artists in caves deep underground (above left) show the kinds of horses living at that time.

The Eohippus, in the foreground left, was the ancestor of the horse. It lived about 50 million years ago. Its descendant the Mesohippus, in the background, was slightly larger and had three toes on each foot.

Man Tames the Horse

For thousands of years, people probably hunted the horse. No one knows exactly where the horse was first domesticated, but since the horse is believed to have originated in North-East Europe and Central Asia, it was probably first tamed by the tribes living there. One of the earliest pictorial records of a man riding a horse exists in the tomb of Horemheb, who ruled Egypt in the 1300s BC.

A relief sculpture of a horse and ▶
rider from a Roman villa in Turkey.

The pharaoh Tutankhamun drives his chariot into battle.

Horses in Ancient Civilisations

Once people discovered how to tame, and particularly how to ride, the horse, they opened up enormous possibilities for their own development. Not only did the horse give them freedom of movement, but a great psychological advantage over people on foot. Even when approaching in peace, the first mounted man must have been an awesome sight to a horseless people.

Certainly, for long periods, the horse was man's partner rather than his servant. In warfare, the capture of good enemy horses was as important as the capture of prisoners. Through wars different types of horses became inter-mixed, the victors not only taking away some of the best, but leaving some of their own behind to breed in the conquered countries. In this way, separate breeds began to come into existence.

Early Horsemanship

The first notable horsemen were the Persians, followed by the Scythians, the Assyrians and the Greeks. As far as we know, it was the Greeks who first took a serious interest in the best way to ride and to train horses. In 365 BC, Xenophon, who was a Greek cavalry officer, compiled books on the art of equitation, the principles of which remain valid to this day. However, he and all other early horsemen laboured under a disadvantage: although bridles and bits were in use, no one had as yet invented the saddle.

Nubian soldiers from the Upper Nile were the first to ride in saddles, which made fighting on horseback very much easier. The cantle gave support against the force of a charging enemy; it also braced the back so that the rider could shoot arrows from a heavy bow. Stirrups came much later, introduced by the Huns of Mongolia in the 4th century AD.

Saddles and stirrups made it easier for ordinary people who

Medieval pilgrims on the way to Canterbury.

were not trained warriors to ride and to use horses for ordinary, every-day purposes, such as going from place to place, going on pilgrimages, or hunting. Also, women, who until then had been either forced to walk or flung up on a horse and carried about in front of the men, could now ride on their own. They began with one stirrup, sitting discreetly sideways, and usually on gentle-paced horses called *amblers*.

Horses were also used to pull fighting chariots. In the 1st century AD, Queen Boadicea is reputed to have driven a three-horse chariot into war in her almost successful battles against the Romans in Britain. In Rome itself during those times, chariot-racing became a sport. It was possibly the first ever equestrian spectator sport, although polo was played long before that in India, many centuries before it was brought to Europe from India by the British colonists.

King John of England stag-hunting in the early 13th century.

The Age of Chivalry

The Age of Chivalry was, literally, the age of the horse, the word 'chivalry' deriving from the French 'cheval', or 'chevallerie'. At first, when lords and knights wore chainmail armour and the horses usually had only head protection, horses could be light and active. In those days the tourneys were affairs of speed, colour and pageantry. As time passed, armour grew heavier and heavier, and the horses as well as the men were almost completely covered with jointed metal plates. Strength in the horse then became all-important; an armoured battle horse, carrying a fully armoured man on top, would be burdened with some 30 stone (190 kg), its rider being hoisted on to its back by crane.

The jousts of those days must have been truly tremendous spectacles: two fully armed knights thundering towards one another on animals similar to the Shire, each trying to tip the other out of the saddle. From very early times, kings and courtiers also rode horses to hunt game of various sorts in the royal parks and demesnes.

French and English knights taking part in a 14th-century tournament.

A highly trained Lipizzaner horse at the Spanish Riding School, Vienna.

Military services, as well as the courts, kept alive the tradition of fine horsemanship for centuries.

The Great Riding Schools

Through the ages, many people rode horses in order to get about, without much thought of how they were riding. Since the time of Xenophon, however, there have always been some people dedicated to the 'art of equitation'.

An early European Master of Equitation was Antoine de Pluvinel (1555-1602), who taught Louis XIII of France. The greatest Master was undoubtedly François de la Guérinière (1688-1751), on whose teachings classical equitation today is founded, and from which sprang the two great European Schools: Saumur in France, and the Spanish Riding School in Vienna. All the movements taught in those schools had a definite purpose at that time, since they made a cavalry horse supple and obedient, and able quickly to evade the action of an enemy.

Apart from these schools, the task of preserving the highest principles of equitation was performed, until the latter half of this century, by the military.

Horses in the New World

The first horses to reach the American continent were Spanish and were taken into both North and South America by the Conquistadores. When the Conquistadores left, many of the horses ran wild, to become in time the mustangs of the North American plains and the founders of the Criollo breed of South America. Many of these horses were captured and domesticated again by the Indians, probably the world's best natural riders. The horse held a place of honour in their lives.

Horses in War

Horses have undoubtedly undergone much suffering in war for mankind's sake. But until World War I, and its horrors of poison gas and high-explosive shells, the horse was still Man's partner in battle; each was dependent on the skill of the other for survival.

Army horses have always been well cared for, and the names of many famous chargers have been immortalised by their devoted owners. The first war-horse known by name to history is Alexander the Great's *Bucephalus*, which no-one else could ride. When he died in 326 BC, Alexander caused the city of Bucephala to be built on the site of his grave. Napoleon's charger, *Marengo*, was a small grey Arab. He carried his master safely through many campaigns, even though Napoleon was not reputed to be an outstanding horseman.

Copenhagen, a chestnut Thoroughbred, reached the climax of his career when he carried the Duke of Wellington throughout the en-

American Indians on a bear hunt. A detail from one of George Catlin's many paintings of Indian life.

tire battle of Waterloo. He later enjoyed a happy retirement at the Duke's home, where even in old age he gave some memorable and exciting rides to those guests privileged to ride him.

Napoleon on Marengo.

The hard life of 19th-century coach horses.

Horses at Work

At the same time that lighter, more aristocratic horses were being developed, the work horses and ponies of the world were playing their part, helping mankind to farm the land and produce food. For many years, in many countries, the ass was mankind's principal worker, both on the land, as a pack animal, and for riding; similarly, that useful hybrid, the mule, which was the result of crossing a Jack donkey with a mare.

In the more remote areas, especially in mountainous regions, ponies rather than horses were used; these tough, hardy animals could withstand severe winters, and periods when there was little food for either Man or beast. In the plains and fertile valleys, the heavy draught horses ploughed and sowed and harvested, and pulled great loads to the towns and cities. In each area, people developed the type of horse or pony (or ass or mule) best suited to the conditions and the work required of it.

The worst time for horses, except for racehorses, which have always been the élite, was the 19th century, when people travelling by coach began to want to travel as fast as possible. Horses pulling stage and mail coaches would be driven to their limits in all weathers and all conditions in order to keep up to almost impossible timetables. Horses used for the fast, timed coaches seldom lasted as much as four years on the job.

It was not much better for the cab horses of the time. Many may have had knowledgeable owners or drivers, but many had not; and they had hard lives working on the slippery city cobbles. Very different were the lives of the private coach and carriage horses of the wealthy, which were well-bred, well fed, and often housed in stables more luxurious than some of today's houses. Yet even they sometimes ended their lives pulling a cab.

Horses in Sport

Horse racing has probably been carried on since the first man sat on a horse or pony and wanted to prove it was faster than his neighbour's. In England, racing became a popular sport in late Tudor times, and was officially recognised in the reign of Charles II, who established a village at Newmarket as racing's headquarters. Trotting races, and matches, have existed in many countries for a long time.

Horses in Today's World

The motor-car and the tractor, combined with man's growing obsession with speed, might well have meant – and nearly did mean – the end of the horse. In most industrialised countries, the horse population dropped alarmingly from the end of World War I until the 1950s. Apart from racehorse breeders, only a few dedicated people kept on breeding horses and ponies, and here and there, a farmer would find it still paid him to work a pair or two of heavy horses.

Today the horse, once Man's partner, then his servant – sometimes his slave – has come into its own again. In most countries of the world, horse and pony breeding have become serious businesses. Horse activities are flourishing as never before, and not only at competitive level. Riding clubs, driving clubs, pony clubs, pony-trekking, holidays on horseback, an infinite number of horse shows, the publicity given to show-jumping on television, not to mention the vast number of books written about the horse, all emphasise the importance of the horse in modern life.

A police horse at work.

Eventing   *A holiday on horseback.*

PRINCIPAL BREEDS

THE ARAB

The Arab is the oldest pure breed in the world. To quote a great authority, Lady Wentworth, 'the Arab is a Tap Root, not derived from anything else at all. It has the gift, possessed alone by true root stock, of absolute dominance in breeding . . . of impressing its own character on any other breed. It is the chief origin of our national racehorse (the Thoroughbred) . . . and of light horse breeds all over the world'.

And yet, no records exist of its own origin, although ancient drawings and carvings prove that it existed long before the Christian era, and before it became the most prized possession of the desert Arabs. Throughout its long history no alien blood has ever been introduced; it has remained entirely and purely itself. To the Arabs it was known as *keheilan,* meaning pure blood through and through, or 'thoroughbred'.

While a good horse or pony of any breed inevitably has a certain beauty of line, the Arab possesses a symmetry of proportion which lifts it above them all, and a pride of bearing comparable to what in humans is called 'star quality'. But the Arab is not only beautiful to look at. It possesses to the full all the qualities most desirable in an equine : soundness of wind, freedom from leg troubles, speed, stamina, and the capacity — belied by its looks — to endure harsh conditions. It has outstanding stamina and strength for its size. It is a light, balanced and comfortable ride, and is capable not only of all the normal activities demanded of a riding horse, but also the less normal, such as endurance, and long-distance riding. Moreover, because for centuries it has shared fully the life of its Arab masters, it has

a unique love of human companionship and a highly developed intelligence. Although full of spirit, it is quick to understand and co-operate with a sympathetic human partner.

Basically, the Arab is a small horse, usually under 15 hh. Breeding for extra height often, though not always, results in a loss of quality and type ; breeders in Poland have produced many excellent Arabs over 15 hh. The Arab's conformation is unique. The head is small, with a dished (concave) profile, tapering to a small muzzle with flexible nostrils, capable of great dilation. The eyes are large, set wide apart, and low in the skull. The ears are small and sharply cut. The neck is arched, and set into the jaw in an arched curve. The withers, which are not high, slope into a strong and level back ; the chest is broad and deep ; the quarters broad and level, with the tail set high and carried gaily. The legs, with iron-hard tendons, have big flat knees, and should have strong hocks. The pasterns are springy, the feet hard and round. The Arab's action is free, straight and fast at all paces. Its colours are bay, grey or chestnut.

The purity of Arabian blood, guarded jealously for so long in the Middle East, is guarded equally so today in the Western world by the Arab Horse Societies in the various countries where Arabs are bred, and also by the World Arab Horse Organisation. Several Arab-type breeds exist which are not pure-breds, notably the Shagya Arabian and the Siglavy Arabian of Hungary, both based on pure stock, but not conforming to the strict pedigree standards needed for recognition as pure-breds, or *keheilans.* The Polish Arab, however, is pure-bred.

The Arab's head has a distinctive concave profile, small muzzle and widely set large eyes.

Arab horses taking part in a ▶ Berber festival in Morocco.

The Arab excels at long-distance and endurance riding, and is exceptionally strong for its size.

THE THOROUGHBRED

The fastest and most valuable horse in the world, the Thoroughbred today races in some 50 countries and is bred in many of them. Every single Thoroughbred in existence traces back to one or other of three Arab stallions imported into England in the late 17th and early 18th centuries.

The first of these, the Byerly Turk, was captured from the Turks in battle by Captain Byerly, who first used him as his charger and then put him to stud in 1690 when he retired from the army. The Byerly Turk is the founder of the Herod line.

The Darley Arabian arrived in 1704, bought by Thomas Darley, at that time consul in Aleppo. His first crop of foals produced the first truly great racehorse: *Flying Childers,* out of *Betty Leedes.* She was herself the daughter of an Arab, the Leedes Arabian, from whom descend all grey Thoroughbreds. The Darley Arabian became the great-great-grandsire of the most famous racehorse of all time: *Eclipse.*

Last to arrive, in 1729, was the Godolphin Arabian, bought in France by Edward Coke, who sold him to Lord Godolphin. At stud, he became the founder of the Matchem line, a branch of which flourishes in the United States today through the fabulously successful *Man o' War.*

The evolution of the breed was remarkably quick. In less than 100 years it was established, its characteristics and abilities unchanged to this day. If a Thoroughbred today can cover a given distance slightly faster than its 19th-century counterpart, it is due rather to improved courses and better horse management than to any actual increase of speed in the animal.

As important as the three founding stallions were the mares they served. Many of these were themselves of Oriental, or part-Oriental, blood. As early as the reign of King John in the 13th century, Eastern horses had been brought into England. From late Tudor times onwards, English monarchs possessed Royal Studs, importing horses from Spain and Italy as well as from the East, while many rich private owners also bred quality stock.

In the second half of the 18th century, breeding, and the keeping of records became more scientific and systematic. In 1773, James Weatherby was appointed 'Keeper of the Match Book' to the Jockey Club, the governing body of racing in Great Britain since 1750. In 1813, Weatherby issued the first General Stud Book, and from that day to this, the firm of Weatherby and Son has been responsible for all pedigree and performance records of Thoroughbreds in Great Britain and Ireland.

The Thoroughbred, however, is not only a racehorse. Its speed, courage, stamina and almost perfect conformation enable it to adapt itself to, and excel at, any form of equestrian sport or activity: steeplechasing, hunting, show-jumping, eventing and dressage. It is, for the experienced rider, the supreme riding horse. Apart from its progenitor, the Arab, no other breed has had a greater or more beneficial influence on the horse and pony breeds of today.

In height, the Thoroughbred ranges from 14.2 to 17 hh, the average being about 16 hh. Its conformation is that of the highest class of equine in existence. The head is refined and well modelled; the neck, elegant and arched. The withers are pronounced; the shoulder very sloping. The back is short, the body deep, the croup high and the quarters generous; the hocks are well let down, the legs clean and hard with good bone, and the tendons pronounced. The action is powerful and long-striding. Any whole colour is permitted.

The fine, intelligent head of the outstanding Thoroughbred steeple-chaser Red Rum.

The fastest breed of ▶ horses in the world: Thoroughbreds at racing pace, with the famous American jockey Willie Shoemaker on the right.

The Thoroughbred, perhaps the most perfect equine conformation.

Finland

THE FINNISH HORSE

The Finnish Horse is a more than usually versatile animal, being used for such different purposes as work on the land, hauling timber, pulling loads, being ridden, going in harness from farm to market, and competing in trotting races. It descends from two closely related breeds: the Finnish Draught, and the Finnish Universal. Both these breeds had admixtures of various warm and cold-blooded types, imported into Finland for crossing with native ponies of the Northern Forest type.

The countryside of Finland is sparsely populated; its agricultural communities are small and often far apart. The Finnish Horse is thus admirably suited to be the general work-horse and pleasure horse of its inhabitants. Standing from 15 to 15.2 hh, and bred for performance rather than looks, the Finnish Horse is perhaps lacking in quality. It is, however, a sturdy, active, well-made animal, with a sensible head, a strong neck, good shoulders and well-

A Finnish Horse at work.

developed quarters. It has good legs, with a short cannon, and excellent bone. It carries very little feather — only a tuft at the fetlock. It has a sound constitution, great stamina, and is a willing worker with a kind temperament. The main colour is chestnut, with a lighter mane and tail.

The North Swedish Horse has many pony characteristics.

Sweden

THE NORTH SWEDISH HORSE

The North Swedish Horse is a light draught horse, evolved by upgrading local stock through crossing, first with Gudbrandsdal ponies from Norway, and later with Oldenburgs. The breed was established in the early years of this century.

Though inheriting size from the Oldenburg, the North Swedish Horse retains a number of pony characteristics. It is hardy, long-lived, economical to keep, strong for its size, and exceptionally resistant to equine diseases. It has a well-shaped head, a strong, fairly short neck, a long, deep body, and short, strong legs with good bone. Its action is free and long-striding, with a particularly good trot. It is a willing, fast worker, used for both farm and forest work. It stands from 15 to 15.3 hh. The usual colours are brown, chestnut and black, though it can also be dun, a colour characteristic of animals carrying native pony blood.

Developed from the North Swedish Horse is the North Swedish Trotter. This is really a lighter version of the breed, selectively bred to develop its natural trotting ability. While not to be compared with the American Standardbred, or the French or Russian Trotters, it is nevertheless a popular harness racehorse, of the same height and colouring as the North Swedish Horse.

THE SWEDISH WARM BLOOD

The Swedish Warm Blood is a riding horse of quality, the result of some 300 years of selective breeding, crossing various cold-blood breeds with warm bloods, principally Anglo-Norman and Hanoverian. Originally, the Swedish Warm Blood was developed to cater for the army's need for good cavalry horses. In recent years, with the growing demand for good all-round riding horses, Thoroughbred, Trakehner and Arab blood has been added.

Standing from 16 to 16.2 hh, the Warm Blood is a strong, sound horse of good conformation, with plenty of depth through the girth, and strong, short legs with good bone. It is up to a fair amount of weight, and has a kindly temperament. It has a particular aptitude for dressage.

The Swedish Warm Blood

Norway
THE GUDBRANDSDAL

This very old breed derives, as do many of the native breeds of Scandinavia and the British Isles, from the North European Forest type of primitive horse. It has many characteristics in common with the Dales Pony. Although the Gudbrandsdal can stand as high as 15 hh, it is nevertheless, in type and character, a pony, endowed with the excellent pony qualities of longevity, hardiness, and the ability to survive on rough pasture and poor rations.

In conformation, the Gudbrandsdal has a neat pony head, a good front, strong shoulders, a deep chest, a longish back and strong legs with a short cannon. It carries a lot of feather, and the mane and tail are luxuriant. The usual colours are black, bay and brown. Its action is free and lively, the trot being particularly active and long-striding. The Gudbrandsdal is used as a riding and general utility animal.

An offshoot of the Gudbrandsdal is the Dole Trotter, a lighter version of the breed, with a little admixture of trotting blood to develop the natural excellence of the Gudbrandsdal's pace. Although the Trotter averages around 15 hh, it also retains many pony characteristics, and is a tough, active harness animal.

The Gudbrandsdal

THE FJORD PONY

Fjord ponies with characteristic two-toned mane and forelock.

Once the mount of the Vikings, the Fjord Pony originated in western Norway, and is now popular all over Scandinavia and in many other countries. It shows its primitive type origin clearly, being always cream dun in colour, with a dark eel stripe along the back, and zebra markings on the legs. The mane and tail colouring is distinctive, and particular to the breed: both are dark in the centre, light cream or silvery to the outside.

The Fjord Pony is hardy, sure-footed and a tireless worker, and in Norway is used extensively for farm work in mountainous districts where it would be impossible to use a tractor. It also has good paces and an exceptionally kind and co-operative temperament, qualities which combine to make it a good all-round riding and trekking pony. It also goes well in harness: some have already made names for themselves in competitive driving events.

In height, the Fjord Pony ranges from 13 to 14.1 hh. The head is rather wide, the ears small, and the eyes wide-set and intelligent. The muzzle is nearly always a paler colour than the coat. The neck is strong and muscled; the body is longish, but deep through the girth; the legs are short and strong, and the feet particularly hard and good. There is little feather — only a silky tuft at the fetlock.

Denmark

THE FREDERIKSBORG

In 1562, King Frederick II of Prussia set up the Royal Frederiksborg Stud. He stocked it first with Andalusians from Spain, then added Neapolitan, Eastern and English blood, thus establishing the Frederiksborg breed. In the days of the great European riding schools, the Frederiksborg was a highly esteemed school horse, as well as being an excellent cavalry charger.

The stud existed until 1839, when it was closed down principally because too many of the best animals had been sold off to upgrade other breeds. Private breeders, however, kept the Frederiksborg breed alive, and today it is popular all over Denmark.

The Frederiksborg is a fine, strong active horse of considerable quality, averaging just under 16 hh. It is deep-chested, with particularly powerful shoulders, good legs with plenty of bone and good action. The predominant colour is chestnut.

THE KNABSTRUP

This breed came into existence by chance. During the Napoleonic wars, Spanish troops were in Denmark for a short time. When they went home, one of their officers left behind a spotted mare. She was bought by a butcher and put to work pulling his delivery cart. A certain Major Villars Lunn, owner of the Knabstrup estate, and a knowledgeable breeder of riding horses, saw the mare and was impressed by her speed and stamina. He bought her, and put her to

a Palomino-coloured Frederiksborg stallion. In 1813, she produced a son, called *Flaebehingsten*, which was spotted, and which became the foundation stallion of the Knabstrup breed.

The mare, called *Flaebehoppen*, was a chestnut, with blanket markings and a white mane and tail. It is interesting to speculate what her ancestry might have been, to have enabled her to pass down spot-patterning through so many generations. She is said to have been of English hunter, rather than Spanish or Eastern, type. The breed which she and her Frederiksborg mate founded produces tough, active riding horses of good conformation, endowed with speed, stamina and good paces.

All the various colours and spot patterns accepted by Appaloosa societies now exist in the Knabstrup.

The Frederiksborg

A group of Knabstrups grazing.

Iceland
THE ICELANDIC PONY

The Icelandic Pony is not indigenous. The first settlers in Iceland were two Norwegian chiefs, named Ingolfur and Leif, who emigrated there in 871, taking with them their families, household goods, and livestock. They were soon followed by other settlers from Norway and from the Western Isles of Britain. The present Icelandic Pony is therefore a mixture of two types: the North European Forest Horse and the Celtic Pony.

For a thousand years, until about 50 years ago, Icelandic Ponies were the only means of transport in Iceland: they were used for riding, as pack ponies, and for draught and agricultural work. In the last century, many were exported to England to work in the coal-mines.

Today, the popularity of pony-trekking holidays has ensured the survival of the breed, and not only for visitors to Iceland. The ponies are exported to, and bred in, a number of other countries to cater for pony-trekking enthusiasts.

Standing from 12 to 13 hh, with occasionally a few bigger ones, the Icelandic Pony is sturdy and stocky, and has a fairly large head; intelligent eyes; a short, thick neck, with a thick, heavy mane and forelock; a deep girth; and strong sound legs. It is tough and docile, possesses very keen sight, and is noted for its homing instinct. It is very strong for its size. The usual riding pace is the *tolt*, a form of amble or lateral trot which is fast and comfortable. Icelandic Ponies can be any colour, though there are many duns and greys.

Icelandic ponies in their natural surroundings — the bleak and treeless landscape of Iceland.

The British Isles
THE HUNTER

The hunter is a type rather than a breed, but it is so well known that it merits inclusion. In fact, it can be said to be accepted as a breed in Britain, where the Hunters' Improvement Society exists for its furtherance. Officially, hunters are divided into weights: light, medium and heavy. Light hunters carry up to 13½ stone (85.7 kg); medium, up to 14½ stone (92 kg); and heavy, any weight upwards. Light and medium hunters are very similar, the medium having a little extra substance. The heavy should also be a quality horse, but it is more difficult to breed good, quality heavies.

While many of the light and medium hunters are Thoroughbreds, the majority are half or three-quarter bred. Many of the best heavyweights come from Ireland and are the result of crossing Thoroughbreds with Irish Draught mares. Many good heavies are also bred by crossing the Cleveland Bay with the Thorough-bred. The Hunters' Improvement Society is an independent body which holds an annual show of Thoroughbred stallions, whose owners wish them to qualify for a Society premium. Those awarded premiums are put to stud in various counties in England, and some in Scotland, serving mares at a fee far lower than would normally be paid for the use of a comparable stallion.

As the prime requisites of a hunter are that it should be able to jump and gallop, it must obviously have good conformation: in particular, good legs with hard, flat bone, strong quarters and well-laid shoulders. The hunter's Thoroughbred blood will ensure that, as well as speed, it has plenty of courage. Many hunters become point-to-pointers, while some graduate to National Hunt racing.

Hunters at a meet being ridden out to hounds.

The type also produces many successful event horses. Hunters can be any whole colour, and in height range from 15.2 hh upwards. Below 15.2 they are classified as small hunters, or ladies' hunters. While not all hunters are of show quality, all are first-class, workmanlike animals in great demand in all equestrian-minded countries.

THE CLYDESDALE

A Clydesdale mare and foal

The Clydesdale is the draught horse of Scotland. The breed was established in the mid-18th century by the farmers of Lanarkshire, who imported Flemish stallions to cross with their lighter native mares. Their aim was to produce animals of greater strength and substance, capable not only of agricultural work, but of hauling the coal from the recently developed Scottish mines.

Although essentially a heavy horse, the Clydesdale is not gross, and can be said to possess more quality than most other draught horses. Not so massive as the Shire, the average height of the Clydesdale is 16.2 hh. For its size and weight it is exceptionally active. Great emphasis has always been placed on breeding animals with sound limbs and good feet, which should be round and

open, with wide, springy hoof-heads.

The head should be wide between the eyes, which should be clear and intelligent. The front of the face is flat: neither dished (concave) nor Roman; the muzzle is wide and the nostrils large. The well-arched neck springs from sloping shoulders and high withers. The body is compact and the thighs packed with muscle. The principal colours are bay, brown and black, with a great deal of white on the legs (which carry abundant feather), on the face, and often on the body as well.

The Clydesdale has a kindly temperament, is easy to handle, and has been exported to many countries. Because of its excellent action, it can produce good weight-carrying riding horses when crossed with the Thoroughbred.

THE SHIRE

One of the largest horses in the world, the Shire is descended, through the Elizabethan Old English Black Horse, from the medieval Great Horses of England. These were animals of great bulk and strength, able to carry into battle knights in full armour weighing up to 30 stone (190 kg). In Elizabethan days and for some time after, powerful horses were needed to pull the heavy, springless carts and coaches over the rough roads of the period, or over country with no roads. These were the fore-bears of the horse which some 200 years ago came to be known as the Shire. Until mechanisation, Shires were England's most popular work-horses; they worked on the land, and pulled drays in the towns and cities.

In height, Shires can stand up to 18 hh, and an average Shire weighs a ton. In spite of their great height and weight, they are exceptionally kind and gentle, and are honest, willing workers. In conformation, they are big-barrelled horses with long legs, carrying a lot of feather. The head is fine in proportion to the size of the horse; the eyes large and kindly; and the ears long, lean and sensitive. The neck is long, slightly arched and well set up to give the horse a command-ing appearance. The shoulder is deep and sloping. The usual colours are bay, brown, black and grey, all the dark colours having liberal white markings on the face and legs.

Recently there has been a great revival of interest in the Shire, and there are increasing numbers of classes for them at agricultural shows. In some parts of the country they still work the land, and several firms of brewers use them to pull their drays in city streets. There would fortunately seem to be no danger of this magnificent breed being allowed to die out.

A team of grey Shires pulling a dray.

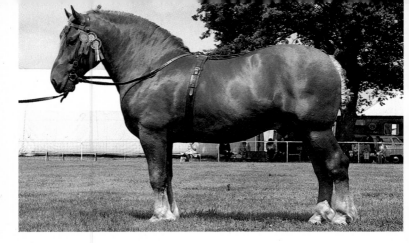

THE SUFFOLK PUNCH

The Suffolk Punch

The Suffolk Punch is a draught horse native to the county of Suffolk on the East Coast of England. According to the historian Camden, Suffolk horses date back to 1506. The Suffolk Punch has several distinctive characteristics. For example, it is always chestnut in colour, the shades varying from dark liver to pale; no other colour is seen. Secondly, it is the only clean-legged British draught horse. Thirdly, every Suffolk Punch today traces back in direct male line to a stallion foaled in 1760.

The Suffolk Punch is a very active horse, and can trot at speeds not to be expected from the Clydesdale or the Shire. Old records show that in the past, weight-pulling trotting contests were very popular. The average height is around 16 hh. In conformation, the body is big, deep and round-ribbed, with great width in front and in the quarters. The head is big, and the forehead wide. The neck is deep at the collar, tapering to a good set of head, and the shoulders are long, sloping and muscular. The legs are straight and strong, the knees big, the hocks long and clean, and the cannon bone particularly short. Being short on the leg gives the horse a low draught, and consequently great pulling power.

The Suffolk Punch is a good-tempered horse and a fast worker. Being clean-legged, it is also very suitable for working the heavy soil of East Anglia, which it still does in many places. It is also used by some brewers as a dray horse. It matures early, is long-lived, and is an economical feeder.

A team of Cleveland Bays competing in a driving event.

THE CLEVELAND BAY

The Cleveland Bay

This is probably the oldest established English breed of horse, originating in the Cleveland district of north-east Yorkshire. In the 17th and 18th centuries it was much used as a pack-horse and was known as Chapman's Horse, packmen and itinerant pedlars of those days being called 'chapmen'. Apart from the introduction of some Thoroughbred blood in the late 18th century, the breed has been free of outside influences. As well as being used for agricultural work in its native Yorkshire, the Cleveland Bay has always been famous as a coach horse. Many European warm-blood breeds have some Cleveland ancestry.

After a period of decline, when only the dedication of a few breeders kept the old blood lines alive, the Cleveland Bay is in great demand again today. This is partly a result of the renewed interest in driving, but also because, when crossed with the Thoroughbred, the Cleveland produces an excellent type of weight-carrying hunter, event horse, and show-jumper.

A handsome, intelligent horse with a sensible temperament, the Cleveland Bay is strong, hardy, long-lived, and possessed of considerable stamina. Standing between 15.3 and 16.2 hh, it is always bay in colour, the only white marking permissible being a small star. The head is large and convex, the neck long and lean. The shoulders are good and the girth deep. The back, though fairly long, is strong, and the quarters powerful. The legs are short and muscular, with good bone, and should carry no superfluous hair, or feather. The Cleveland Bay's action is level, free and long-striding.

43

THE IRISH DRAUGHT HORSE

'Draught' is a slightly misleading term for this excellent Irish horse, which is better described as an all-purpose animal. It has been used as such by Irish farmers for generations — for working the land, going in harness, and on occasions carrying an enthusiastic owner to hounds. Because the type of land varies in different parts of Ireland, there tended for some time to be considerable type-variations within the breed known as Irish Draught. Since the formation of the Irish Draught Stud Book in 1917, the breed-type has become established.

With the coming of mechanisation the Irish Draught went into a long period of decline. Now, however, its breeding is encouraged by the Irish

An Irish Draught mare and her foal

Horse Board, which awards valuable premiums and prizes to good stallions, mares, and foals — a far-sighted policy because the Irish Draught-Thoroughbred cross has produced many of the hunters for which Ireland is famous, and many international showjumpers. But for cross-breeding, good purebreds are necessary and today, with the Horse Board's help, Irish breeders can afford to rear high-class stock.

In height, the Irish Draught stands between 15 and 17 hh. It has a keen, alert outlook; excellent shoulders; and a powerful frame set on strong, muscular limbs. The cannon bone is short, the forearm and second thigh, strongly muscled. The Irish Draught can carry a little hair on the fetlocks, but is generally clean-legged. The principal colours are bay, brown, chestnut, black and grey. The action is free and straight, and most Irish Draughts are natural jumpers.

THE CONNEMARA PONY

A Connemara Pony under saddle.

The Connemara is one of the oldest equine inhabitants of the British Isles, being a descendant of the Celtic Pony, one of the early primitive breeds of Europe. Through the centuries the breed has had admixtures of Spanish (Andalusian) and Arab blood, but since the establishment of the Connemara Pony Breeders' Society in 1928, the policy has been, by careful and selective breeding, to maintain the breed intact. Although native to Ireland, the Connemara is now widely bred throughout Great Britain, and there is one large stud in France.

The Connemara is one of the most versatile of the native pony breeds. Its good temperament makes it an excellent riding pony for children, and suitable for taking part in competitive show-jumping and junior eventing. Because the breed has plenty of bone and substance and its height range is from 13 to 14.2 hh, the Connemara can also be ridden by adults. When crossed with the Thoroughbred, the result is an excellent riding horse, with the quality of the Thoroughbred allied to the sagacity, sure-footedness and hardiness of the good pony.

In type, the Connemara is a true pony, with a neat quality head; a well-arched neck; sloping shoulders; a compact body with a deep girth; and short legs with clean, hard, flat bone. It has great stamina and is hardy, tractable and intelligent; and a naturally good jumper. The most usual colour today is grey, with some bays and browns and an occasional black. The most typical, however, is the original somewhat yellowish dun, which is a particular feature of the breed.

THE DALES PONY

The Dales Pony is a native of the area to the east of the Pennines of northern England. Because of its ability to carry heavy weights, it was widely used as a pack pony in the lead mines of Northumberland and Durham. It could be seen transporting loads weighing up to 16 stone (100 kg) from the workings to the docks, a distance of some 40 miles 64 km) a day. This feat of endurance earned the Dales Pony a reputation for sturdiness, soundness and willingness to work.

About 100 years ago, a Welsh Cob stallion was used extensively on Dales mares, and he passed on many of his characteristics to his descendants, notably an ability to trot fast and freely with good straight action. Essentially an all-purpose pony that can be ridden, driven, or worked on the land, its numbers were declining dangerously until fairly recently. However, it is now coming back into popularity as an excellent trekking pony. Dales mares have also been successfully crossed with Thoroughbreds, producing sturdy, active, courageous horses that have done well in pony and riding club activities. So, hopefully, another ancient breed has been saved from extinction.

Dales average around 14.1 hh in height, and are usually black or dark brown in colour, though there are occasional greys. In conformation, the head is neat and pony-like, with a fine jaw and throat. The neck is inclined to be short and the shoulder sometimes straight; but the back, loins and quarters are excellent; the ribs are well-sprung; and the feet, legs and joints are good, the pony having great bone for its size. Mane and tail hair is luxuriant, and the legs carry a lot of feather. Dales ponies are docile, sure-footed, and easy to break and handle.

A Dales Pony stallion

THE FELL PONY

At one time, the Fell and the Dales ponies were virtually the same breed, the difference of name being purely territorial, the Fell inhabiting the west side of the Pennine Hills and the mountainous regions of Cumbria. During the last century Fells, like the Dales, were doing the same work of carrying lead to the docks. But whereas the Dales have had admixtures of outside blood (probably some cart-horse as well as Welsh Cob), Fell breeders have always zealously guarded the purity of the breed. Few Mountain and Moorland ponies of today breed truer to type than the Fell. However, Fell mares have also been successfully crossed with Thoroughbreds.

Though smaller than the Dales, ranging from 13 to 14 hh, the Fell Pony is equally tough, sound and hardy, and has the advantage of a better riding shoulder. It makes a good driving as well as riding pony, is extensively used for trekking, and is versatile enough to go hunting in rough country. Being sure-footed and sensible, it makes an excellent mount for the elderly enthusiast.

In conformation, the Fell has a typical pony-type head, with neat, well-placed ears. The neck is of good length, with a definite crest; the shoulder well laid-back; the girth deep; the legs good, with a short cannon; the knees big and well developed; and the hocks well let-down. Mane and tail hair is abundant and distinctly curly, and a fair amount of feather is carried. The usual colours are black, dark brown and dark bay, with an occasional grey, but the most favoured colour is black.

A Fell Pony in a driving class at a show.

THE DARTMOOR PONY

Today, much of Dartmoor, in Devonshire, is still the same open, uncultivated moorland that has been inhabited for centuries by Dartmoor ponies. The breed has had some infusions of alien blood, but for many years now, breeders have concentrated on keeping it pure and true to its original type.

Like all Mountain and Moorland ponies, Dartmoors are exceptionally hardy, being able to survive in harsh

The head of a Dartmoor Pony.

Ponies on Dartmoor

conditions and on scant fodder. They make excellent children's riding ponies, being narrow, friendly and willing, and many are natural jumpers. They are also strong enough to carry adults with ease and spirit, and in their home district, often do so.

In height, Dartmoors must not exceed 12.2 hh. Brown, bay and black are the preferred colours, though all but piebald and skewbald are allowed. They have quality heads; very small and alert ears; strong, but not heavy, necks; and well-muscled backs, loins and quarters. Their action is true riding action: low and free. Dartmoors are often used as foundation stock for the breeding of Riding ponies, and there are Dartmoor studs in France as well as Britain.

THE EXMOOR PONY

Indigenous to Exmoor, in the south-west of Devon and Somerset, the Exmoor Pony is believed to be the only native breed to be descended more or less unchanged from its primitive ancestor, the Celtic Pony. It is already mentioned as a distinct breed in the Domesday Book of 1065.

Exmoors have many distinctive characteristics. While they can be bay, brown, or mouse dun, all have mealy, light-coloured muzzles and the same mealy colour under the belly and between the thighs. The eye has a very heavy top lid, giving a hooded effect, known locally as a 'toad eye'. The tail has a thick fan-like growth of hair at the top, and the winter coat has a unique texture: short, thick, springy, and virtually waterproof.

Exmoors are strong, hardy and possessed of great stamina. While they make good children's ponies, they are also capable of carrying adults. Their conformation is excellent, being deep-chested, with good shoulders; strong backs, loins and quarters; short, clean legs with good bone; and neat, hard feet. Like the Dartmoor, the Exmoor is used as foundation stock for Riding ponies. The height limit of the Exmoor is 12.2 hh for mares, 12.3 hh for stallions.

Exmoor ponies in their natural surroundings.

THE NEW FOREST PONY

Although ponies are known to have lived wild in the New Forest since the 10th century, they have had so many different infusions of blood that it has been difficult to breed a fixed type of New Forest Pony. That they may vary in height from 12.1 to 14.2 hh is to their advantage; the larger ones are true family ponies, being suitable for parents as well as for children to ride.

New Forest Ponies may be of any colour except piebald or skewbald, though bays and browns predominate. They are docile, tractable, and easy to break and handle. Centuries of having to struggle for existence in the wild have made them intelligent and resourceful.

The selective breeding of recent years has made the New Forest a pony of quality. The shoulder is good and the action free and straight, and there is great depth through the heart. The breed is fast becoming one of the most popular of all native breeds, and many ponies are exported to countries all over the world.

A New Forest mare and foal.

THE HIGHLAND PONY

The Highland Pony is the largest of the British Mountain and Moorland breeds, and is of great antiquity, being descended from a probable mixing of the Forest Horse and the Celtic Pony. Highlands have also had some infusion of Arab blood. The breed is native to the Highlands of Scotland and several of the islands off the Scottish west coast.

For centuries Highlands were used as all-purpose ponies by Scottish crofters, being driven and ridden as well as being used on the land. Later, they were used — and still are— as hill ponies, taking shooters or stalkers up the hills, or bringing the deer down slung across their backs on special deer saddles. The Highland Pony might never have become known outside its native country had it not been for pony-trekking, which can be said to have begun in Scotland. Now they have become popular all over Britain and have been exported to other countries.

When properly broken and well fed, Highland ponies give as good a ride as any of the large native breeds.

Highland ponies in wild Scottish countryside.

They are sensible, active and sure-footed, and some have a quite surprising ability to jump. They also go well in harness. Being extremely strong for their size, they make good family ponies, able to carry adults as well as children.

In height, Highlands can vary from 13 to 14.2 hh. In conformation, the head is well modelled, with small ears, large eyes, and wide nostrils capable of dilation. The neck is fairly long and crested; the back short; the ribs well sprung and the chest deep; the quarters powerful and the thighs well muscled. The bone is flat and hard. The mane and tail hair is luxuriant, soft and silky, and the legs carry a silky fringe of feather.

The colours are all shades of dun, from grey through golden to a dark mouse. Brown, bay and black are old colours and not so usual, while some island ponies are liver chestnut, with light manes and tails. White markings are not allowed, except for a small star. The eel stripe is common, and many ponies have zebra markings on the legs.

THE SHETLAND PONY

Apart from the Argentinian Falabella, which is really a 'trick' breed, the Shetland is the smallest of all ponies. It is also the strongest member of the equine family in relation to its size. Native to the Shetland Islands, off the north coast of Scotland, its definite origin is unknown. It may have been introduced in the distant past from Scandinavia and crossed later with mainland Celtic ponies.

In the past, the ponies did all the work that needed to be done on the islands. As there was no other means of transport, the Shetlanders also rode them. In the last century, they were bred extensively to work in the coal-mines of northern England, many of the best stock leaving the islands at this time. Today there are again good herds on Shetland, but the ponies are also bred abroad.

Provided they are not allowed to get too fat, Shetlands make excellent first ponies for children, for when handled and broken, they are sensible, tractable and companionable. They also go well in harness.

The height of Shetlands is measured in inches: it should be not more than 40 inches for mares, 42 for stallions. In conformation, the Shetland has a head that is small and refined, and carried high; small ears; large eyes; and wide nostrils. It also has a relatively long, strong neck; pronounced withers; short back, deep through the girth; sloping shoulders; well-sprung ribs; and strong quarters. The strong legs have a long forearm and thigh and a very short cannon with flat bone. The forelock, mane and tail hair is soft and luxuriant, and there is a little hair on the heels. The fashionable colour is black, but Shetlands can be any colour, including piebald and skewbald.

Shetland ponies on the island of Moussa in the Shetlands.

THE WELSH MOUNTAIN PONY

Welsh ponies are divided into four sections, of which the oldest is the Welsh Mountain (Section A). These ponies, much resembling miniature Arabians, have roamed the mountains of Wales and the Borders since long before Roman times. Julius Caesar founded a stud of them in Merionethshire, and was the first to introduce Oriental blood. Arabian blood was added in the 19th century.

Intelligent, strong and hardy, these little ponies are perhaps the most beautiful of all native breeds. They are in great demand as children's riding ponies, and as foundation stock for Riding ponies and for the Welsh sections B and C.

The height limit of the Welsh Mountain Pony is 12 hh. The head is distinctly Arabian, with a dished (concave) profile, wide-set eyes and a tapering muzzle. These ponies have good shoulders, strong backs and graceful necks. The tail is set high and carried gaily, and their action is spectacular. Any colour except piebald and skewbald is allowed.

A team of grey Welsh Mountain ponies taking part in a driving event at a show.

The Welsh Section B, the riding pony of Wales.

limit being 13.2 hh. Although bred to have more of a riding pony than a native pony appearance, their basic native characteristics of hardiness and substance should not be lost. Their conformation, therefore, should be similar to, if a little less sturdy than, that of the Mountain ponies, and the action flatter and less flamboyant.

THE WELSH SECTION C

This splendid little pony, which must not exceed 13.2 hh in height, is also based on the Mountain Pony. It can be described as either a slightly cobbier version of the Mountain Pony, or a smaller, lighter and finer form of the big Welsh Cob. Full of character, gaiety, energy and courage, it makes an ideal hunter for a child or a light adult; it also has a very good reputation as a driving pony. Although, as yet, possibly the least well known of the four Welsh types, the Section C is perhaps the most versatile and useful of them all.

The Welsh Section C, a pony of cob type: one of the best of its breed.

THE WELSH SECTION B

The Welsh Section B is the riding pony of Wales, and is based on the Mountain Pony, crossed perhaps with Section C, or with an Arab or small Thoroughbred. They are taller than the Mountain ponies, their height

THE WELSH COB (SECTION D)

The breeding of these magnificent animals has been a tradition among Welsh farmers for many centuries. They were based originally on the Welsh Mountain Pony and the Old Welsh Cart-horse. Welsh Cobs have always been famous for their trotting ability and have influenced many of the trotting breeds of the world. But they can also gallop and jump, and they make excellent saddle horses and hunters. Welsh Cob teams can also hold their own against all comers in driving events.

In height, Welsh Cobs can range from 14 to 15.2 hh, but however large, they should have the alert, quality, pony-type heads characteristic of all the Welsh types. The body should be deep-girthed, the chest broad and deep, the quarters immensely powerful, and the legs short and strong, with only a tuft of silky hair at the heels. Mane and tail hair should be fine and silky. Like other Welsh ponies, the Cob is hardy, generous and tractable, but full of courage, energy and fire. Also like other Welsh types, it can be of any colour except piebald or skewbald.

THE RIDING PONY

The Riding Pony is a fairly recent breed that has been developed in order to produce small, quality animals of show standard, yet capable of being ridden by children. Evolved mainly by crossing native pony mares, mostly Welsh, Dartmoor or, sometimes, Exmoor, with small Thoroughbred or Arab stallions, the breed is now firmly established, with its own Stud Book and its own Riding Pony stallions.

The breeding of these ponies is a matter of great skill; too much Thoroughbred blood, and they become little horses; too much Arab,

The Riding Pony

A team of Welsh Cobs taking part in a competition.

and the Arabian characteristics are too dominant. Sooner or later, some native blood probably has to be re-infused to keep their true pony character.

In conformation, Riding ponies are truly beautiful little animals, with small quality heads; large, wide-spaced eyes and small, alert ears. They also have graceful necks, and good riding shoulders. They are deep through the girth, and close-coupled, while the quarters are well muscled and the tail is set and carried high. The legs are clean, the cannons short and the bone hard and flinty. Action is straight and free from the shoulder, the hocks well engaged behind. Nevertheless, they remain true ponies, intelligent and alert, and keen but well-mannered rides. They are capable of giving a lot of pleasure to their child riders, as well as winning rosettes for them in the show-ring.

Riding ponies are divided into three heights: 12.2 hh and under; up to 13.2 hh, and up to 14.2 hh, the best of the latter often commanding prices not far off those of racing Thoroughbreds. They can be any whole colour.

57

THE HACKNEY HORSE AND PONY

The Hackney Horse derives from the Norfolk Roadster, a renowned trotting breed of the 18th century. The Roadster was a powerful animal with immense stamina; the most famous one, the *Norfolk Cob*, is reputed to have trotted 24 miles (39 km) in an hour. The best Roadsters were descended from a horse called *Shales*, a grandson of the Thoroughbred *Flying Childers*, himself the son of the Darley Arabian. The Hackney, therefore, carries both Arab and Thoroughbred blood.

With the coming of the railways in the 19th century, the Roadster breed fell into disuse, to be revived, fortunately, by the Hackney Horse Society in the spirited, elegantly actioned horse known today as the Hackney.

The Hackney Horse measures from 14.3 hh upwards, sometimes reaching 16.2 hh. In conformation, the head should be small and concave, with a small muzzle. The neck is fairly long and thick-set; the shoulders powerful, the withers low. The body is compact and not very deep-chested; the legs short and strong; the hocks very well let-down; and the tail set, and carried high.

The most distinctive characteristic of the Hackney is its action, which is very free from the shoulder, the forelegs being thrown both high and well forward, with a slight pause of the foot at each stride giving a distinct 'moment of suspension', when the horse appears to float over the ground. The action of the hindlegs is similar, to a lesser degree.

The Hackney Pony is said to have originated from a small Hackney stallion called *St George*, foaled in 1866. In height, it must be under 14.2 hh, and in type and character it must be true pony, not just a small horse. Its action is even more extravagant than that of the Hackney

Horse. The knees are raised to the highest possible extremity, while the hocks are brought right under the body, and raised almost to touch it.

The usual colours of both the Hackney Horse and the Pony are bay,

A Hackney Horse in harness.
Driven by Mrs. Frank Haydon.

brown, black, and chestnut. Both are seen mostly today in the show-ring, where they are as enthusiastically received as the show-jumpers. Both are also successfully driven in competitive events.

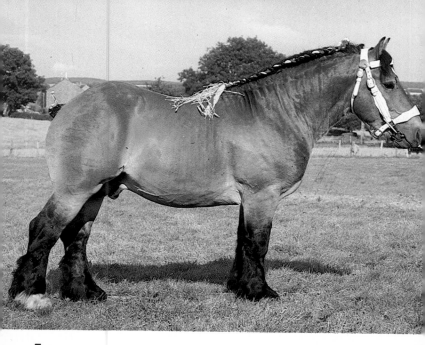

France
THE ARDENNAIS

The Ardennais is an ancient breed of cob-type draught horse, originating in the mountainous district of the Ardennes, bordering France and Belgium. It is thought to be descended from the light draught horses praised by Julius Caesar in his account of the conquest of Gaul.

Because of its great powers of endurance and its docility, combined with a lively temperament, the Ardennais has been of great military service to France. In the Napoleonic wars, the Ardennais distinguished itself in the Russian campaign by enduring the appalling winter conditions better than any other breed. Ardennais were also used as artillery horses in World War I.

The breed is also very popular in Belgium, where some crossing with the Brabançon has tended to increase its size. Ardennais are also bred and worked in Sweden. In France, the survival of the breed is ensured by the French National Studs, at many of which good Ardennais stallions are kept.

The Ardennais varies in height from 14.2 to 15.3 hh, and its conformation is essentially cobby — that is, it has a strong, compact body with a well-rounded rib cage and rounded and muscular quarters, and short legs with excellent bone. The head is well shaped, the ears small, and the outlook alert. The neck is well arched and springs from a sloping shoulder, which ensures the free, level action that gave this breed rather more versatility than that of many other draught breeds. The usual colours are roan, bay and chestnut, with roan predominating.

THE BOULONNAIS

The Boulonnais originates in northern France, and is an unusual draught horse in that during its early history it had considerable infusions of Arab and Barb blood from stallions brought from the East by French Crusaders. Although the Boulonnais is a genuine heavy draught horse, this ancestry has endowed it not only with good action, but with the ability to move fast. At one time it was much used as a carriage horse, where strength and speed were necessities. It was also used to move heavy loads of fish and shellfish quickly from the coast to Paris.

The Boulonnais is a very big, heavy horse, standing between 16 and 17 hh. Nevertheless, in spite of its massive size, it has that touch of quality which has made breeders of draught horses say that a dash of Boulonnais blood in other draught breeds has much the same effect as that of the Thoroughbred on riding horses. In the world of today, there is relatively little use for heavy draught horses. It is fortunate therefore, that the French National Studs are not allowing this ancient and impressive breed to become extinct.

The predominant colour of the Boulonnais is grey, though bay and chestnut are allowed.

The Boulonnais

A team of three Percherons at the French National Stud, Haras du Pin.

The Breton

THE PERCHERON

Of all breeds of heavy draught horses, the Percheron is probably the best known and most widely dispersed throughout the world. It owes its origin to a group of farmers in the La Perche district of northern France — hence the name. It is a mixture of races, with an infusion of Arab blood. The Percheron Society and Stud Book were formed and started in 1882.

Originally produced not only for agricultural work but also for pulling heavy coaches and for artillery work, the Percheron is a draught horse of outstanding quality. It is active, and has considerable grace of movement for so big an animal; some can weigh a ton.

Standing between 16 and 17 hh, the Percheron is well-proportioned, deep-bodied and short-legged, with hard, flinty bone and good, hard feet. Like the British Suffolk Punch, it carries little or no feather. Its colours are grey and black only. The breed was introduced to Britain in 1916, and there is now also a British Percheron Society.

THE BRETON

This is an old breed, native to Brittany. In the Middle Ages it existed in two distinct types: the heavier draught and work-horse, and the lighter saddle horse, or *ambler*. Some outside blood — Norfolk Trotter and Thoroughbred — was introduced in the 18th century.

The Breton of today is a strong, compact, cobby, light draught horse. It is also active, of good temperament, and an excellent all-round worker for the small farmer. Usually standing around 15 hh, it has a fairly short neck, a well-rounded rib cage, and well-developed, muscular quarters. The usual colours are chestnut, and red and blue roan; sometimes bay and black are seen. Its descent from primitive horses is often revealed by the presence of a dark cross on the withers.

THE COMTOIS

This very ancient breed is native to the area bordering on Switzerland, where it is said to have existed since the 6th century, and to have descended from German horses. It is an active, alert, cobby, light draught horse; or alternatively, a cob-type, weight-carrying saddle horse.

In appearance, the Comtois is very similar to the horses which were used in the armies of Louis XIV, and to many depicted in old tapestries. Usually slightly under 15 hh, it has the cob characteristics of rounded rib cage, strong quarters, and short strong legs carrying a little feather. Its colouring is a distinctive chestnut, often a very dark chestnut, almost the colour of plain chocolate; the mane and tail are light-coloured. Like all cobs, it is hardy, a good doer, and a willing worker.

A pair of Comtois mares

THE ANGLO-NORMAN

Normandy is, and always has been, a great horse-breeding centre. The climate is mild, and the soil rich in lime, which encourages the growth of good, sound bone. The Anglo-Norman breed goes back to the Norman Horse of the 11th century, which was strong and enduring, and much prized as a war-horse. William the Conqueror took many of them to England, thereby improving the English horses of that time. Later, the Norman Horse deteriorated by being crossed with draught horses, but in the 18th century, Arab and Thorough-bred blood was introduced.

In the 19th century, a large admixture of Norfolk Trotter blood from England produced the Anglo-Norman Trotter, a versatile, very active harness or saddle horse, with stamina and good bone and muscle. Now known as the Anglo-Norman, the breed has been found to be useful as a blood-outcross for other breeds, and as foundation stock in the formation of new breeds, notably the French Saddle Horse.

The Anglo-Norman of today is a strong, impressive animal, up to weight, and with considerable presence. It has good shoulders, and a long, free-striding, straight action. The average height is around 16 hh and the usual colours are chestnut, bay and brown.

THE ANGLO-ARAB

The term 'Anglo-Arab' means a horse that combines Thoroughbred and Arab blood to the exclusion of any other. Anglo-Arabs are bred in many countries, but nowhere better or more consistently than in France. This is because the French National Studs have been involved in their breeding since the middle of the 19th century, and in over 100 years, have succeeded in stabilising this combination of two of the world's best breeds. The Anglo-Arab is a horse of great quality, capable of holding its own in all types of equestrian sport.

The French Anglo-Arab must possess at least 25 per cent Arab

The Anglo-Norman

The Anglo-Arab

blood; the most usual method of breeding is to put a pure-bred Arab stallion to a Thoroughbred or Anglo-Arab mare. While it is possible to produce what are officially Anglo-Arabs simply by crossing an Arab with a Thoroughbred, the results will not necessarily be so successful as those obtained by over a century of selective breeding.

In conformation, the Anglo-Arab should combine the characteristics of both breeds without unduly displaying those of either, though it will show rather more of the classical Arabian head. It combines the speed of the Thoroughbred with the endurance and the generally more amenable temperament of the Arab. It stands between 15.3 and 16.3 hh, and its usual colours are bay, brown and chestnut.

THE FRENCH TROTTER

A harness racehorse of world quality, the French Trotter, like the American Standardbred, carries a considerable amount of Thoroughbred blood, but was developed from different origins. The foundation stock was Norman mares: these were mated not only with English Thoroughbreds, but with half-bred stallions and with Norfolk Roadsters, the forerunners of the Hackney. Two English horses foaled in the early 19th century had a particular influence on the breed: *Young Rattler,* and *The Heir of Linné.* The great majority of today's Trotters trace back to five sons of those two stallions: *Conquérant, Lavater, Normand, Phaeton,* and *Fuchsia.*

Recently, some Standardbred blood has been introduced, but the French Trotter remains a rather bigger, more raw-boned type of horse than the Standardbred. This is to its advantage,

The head of a French Trotter

A bay French Trotter mare trotting.

because in France ridden trotting races are still popular, and for these a horse must not only be fast, but also have considerable substance and toughness.

Trotters stand between 16 and 16.2 hh. They have the typically sloping quarters of the trotting horse, and good, strong, durable legs.

THE FRENCH SADDLE HORSE

The French Saddle Horse is a composite breed of recent origin, produced principally by crossing the Anglo-Norman with the Thoroughbred. Since 1965, it has had its own section in the Anglo-Norman Stud Book, and its own French Saddle stallions. Entry into the Stud Book, however, is not confined only to the progeny of two French Saddle Horse parents. A foal born to a Thoroughbred mare by a French Saddle stallion, or vice-versa, is equally designated a French Saddle Horse.

The breed can be very fairly compared to the English hunter in that there are variations of height, weight, and to a certain extent, type within it. Also, the basic requirements of each are much the same. They must be quality riding horses of good conformation and temperament, with a fair turn of speed and the ability to jump, so that they are suitable both for the various competitive equestrian sports and for enjoyable riding by less ambitious riders.

Like the English hunters, there are also French Saddle Horses to suit all shapes, sizes and weights of riders. In character, they are honest, game and courageous horses. Standing from 15.2 to 16.3 hh, they can be any whole colour, but chestnut predominates at the moment.

A grey French Saddle Horse leading a bay Anglo-Arab.

THE CAMARGUAIS

The origin of these romantic little horses, known as the 'White Horses of the Sea', is obscure. Some claim them to be indigenous; others, that they descend from Eastern horses. Their home is the Camargue, an area of salty marsh and swampland in the Rhône delta of southern France, between the town of Aiguë Morte and the sea. Here they exist on a diet of rough grass and salt water, and as a result are incredibly tough and hardy. Usually standing under 15 hh, they are strong and active, with a high-stepping walk, a fast gallop, and a notable ability to turn and twist

quickly. They are often used to work the black bulls of the Camargue, which are reared there for the bullring.

The conformation of Camarguais horses is not particularly good. They have rather large heads and straight shoulders, but they have depth through the girth, short, strong backs, and good legs with plenty of bone;

The Camarguais, the White Horse of the Sea, in its natural environment.

their feet are hard and durable. Although the foals are usually born dark, the adult coat colour is always grey, growing whiter with age. At the present time there are about 30 herds in existence.

The Brabançon

Belgium
THE BRABANÇON

The heavy draught horse of Belgium, the Brabançon has been selectively bred for many centuries. Its blood has helped the formation of many other draught horse breeds, including, from Brabançons imported into Britain, the English Shire.

Standing from 16 to 17 hh high, the Brabançon is a heavy, strong horse with great pulling power, but it is handsome as well as powerful. The head is relatively small, finely modelled and well-set on to an arched neck. Its body is compact, and the legs are short with good hard bone. The Brabançon carries a considerable amount of feather. It is a willing, active worker with a particularly good walk, and has a sound constitution. The most usual colours are red roan with dark points, and chestnut; though there are occasional bays, browns, greys and duns.

The Gelderland

The Netherlands
THE GELDERLAND

The Gelderland of today derives from a very old breed of light draught horse native to the Dutch province of Gelderland. In the last century, carriage horses were bred from imported stallions of various breeds, including Thoroughbred, Arab, Holstein, Hackney, Oldenburg and Friesian. Their somewhat varied offspring were all good harness horses and, before the days of the motor car, were popular in many countries.

In this century, some Anglo-Norman blood has been added, and the main consideration of breeders has been consolidation of type. In this, they have been very successful. The modern Gelderland is a strong, active animal of excellent conformation, with great presence and stylish action. It is much sought after by driving enthusiasts, and does extremely well in competitions up to international level. It is also a good saddle horse, and some are fine show-jumpers.

The height range of the Gelderland is from 15.2 to 16 hh. The principal

colours are grey and chestnut, the chestnuts often having a considerable amount of white on the face and legs. Type is now so well established that it is not difficult to find matched pairs, or even teams. To see a team of these stylish, high-couraged horses in action is an exciting experience.

THE FRIESIAN

The Friesian is one of Europe's oldest breeds and is indigenous to the province of Friesland, where draught horses of distinctive type have existed for over 900 years. Throughout the 17th century, Friesians were very popular both as agricultural work-horses, and as weight-carrying saddle horses. As well as being strong and having excellent active paces, they have always enjoyed the reputation of being particularly docile, willing, and easy to handle, even by quite inexperienced people. They are also economical to keep, being good doers, and keeping fit on less food than many other breeds.

In the 19th century, when trotting races became fashionable, the Friesians' free, fast trot enabled them to

The Friesian has many characteristics similar to the British Fell and Dales ponies.

become successful competitive trotters. This, however, tended to make breeders try to produce animals of lighter type, which could have led to the deterioration of the breed. Fortunately a breeding policy was adopted in time; in 1879 the Stud Book was founded and, to be accepted into it, animals not only had to be pedigreed, but also had to comply with high standards of conformation.

Today, Friesians are flourishing as harness horses, and agricultural work-horses. Because of their tractability, Friesian stallions are also used as circus horses.

The Friesian stands around 15 hh, and is a most attractive horse, with a finely moulded head set on a shapely neck; a strong back; and a deep, well-rounded rib-cage. The legs are short, with good bone, and carry a lot of feather; both tail and mane are luxuriant, the mane often reaching almost to the ground. The colour is always black, the only white permissible being a small star. That Friesians are always true colour is proof of the long stabilisation of the breed and of the purity of its lineage.

71

THE DUTCH DRAUGHT HORSE

The Dutch Draught Horse is one of the most massive breeds of Europe and is widely used in Holland for agricultural work on all types of land. Its origin goes back to the middle of the last century. Since 1925, breed characteristics have been stabilised by allowing no horse of unknown pedigree to be entered in the Stud Book.

The Dutch Draught is docile, willing, courageous and intelligent. It is an economical feeder and has a very long working life. In height, it stands up to 16.3 hh, and in conformation it is a deep-bodied animal of heavy build. The neck is short, the head not too heavy, the withers not pronounced and the shoulders somewhat loaded. The back is strong and wide, the ribs well-sprung, and the quarters wide and powerful. The tail is low-set, the croup notably sloping. The legs are strongly muscled, and the feet good. The Dutch Draught Horse is much more active than might be supposed from its weight.

The usual colours of the Dutch Draught are bay, chestnut or grey.

THE GRONINGEN

The Groningen derives from the German Oldenburg, which in turn derives from the Friesian. It was bred to be an all-purpose animal, capable of working on the land and of being both ridden and driven, and was for many years a popular carriage horse. It has an equable temperament, is easily handled, and is an economical feeder — traits inherited from its Friesian forebears. In height, the Groningen stands from 15.2 to 16 hh. It has a quality head and neck, great depth of girth, powerful shoulders and quarters, and short, strong legs.

With today's renewed interest in driving, the Groningen is probably

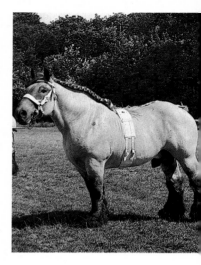

The Dutch Draught Horse

due for a well-deserved revival of popularity, for it is a speedy horse with stylish action and a sound constitution.

The usual colours of the Groningen are bay, dark brown and black.

A young and an older Groningen mare. The dark-coloured one will lighten as it grows older.

Germany

The Trakehner

THE TRAKEHNER

This is undoubtedly the best German breed, and was originally known as, and is still sometimes called, the East Prussian Horse. It takes its name from the Trakehnen Stud, founded in 1732 by King Frederick William I of Prussia. He provided both the land and the foundation breeding stock, partly from existing Royal Studs, and partly by importing high-class Arabs.

As time went on, more Thoroughbred stallions were used; one of them was *Perfectionist,* by *Persimmon*, winner of the English Derby for King Edward VII when he was Prince of Wales.

At the original Trakehnen Stud, four-year-old horses were subjected to rigorous trials, only the best being kept for breeding. Throughout the 250 years of its existence, the Trakehner has been bred with systematic thoroughness, so that today it is a saddle horse of highest quality.

Standing between 16 and 16.2 hh, the Trakehner is a beautiful and good-tempered horse, endowed with stamina and a lively but kind disposition. Its conformation is excellent — as it should be, with the best of Thoroughbred and Arabian blood in its veins. It can be of any whole colour.

The Trakehner is now bred privately in many parts of Germany, and has greatly influenced the Polish Wielkopolski. Trakehners often make top-grade show-jumpers; one with a world-wide reputation was *Halla*, the mare ridden to so many successes by Hans Günther Winkler.

THE HANOVERIAN

The Hanoverian is the best known of the German warm-blood breeds, and owes its origin to the interest taken by the British Hanoverian kings in the horses of their native Hanover. George I sent many English Thoroughbred stallions out to be mated with local mares, which were of varying types. Some of these were descended from the German Great Horse of the Middle Ages, which was the principal war-horse of Europe's armed chivalry. George II of England established the Landesgestut at Celle in 1735, where Holstein as well as Thoroughbred stallions were kept.

For many years the aim of the stud was to produce all-purpose horses for riding, driving and draught work. Since World War II, however, breeding has concentrated on the production of good competition horses, and some Trakehner as well as more Thoroughbred blood has been introduced. The Hanoverian of today is a very successful dressage horse and show-jumper.

Standing from 16 to 17 hh high, the Hanoverian is a strong upstanding animal, up to weight, active and bold, with the courage — but not the speed — of the Thoroughbred. It is of good conformation, if perhaps a little plain. It may be of any whole colour, the most usual being bay, brown, chestnut and black.

THE HOLSTEIN

A slightly heavier stamp of horse than the Hanoverian, the Holstein has a long history tracing back to the 14th century, when it was a weight-carrying war-horse. Spanish and Eastern blood was then brought in to lighten it. In the 19th century, to upgrade the breed still further, Thoroughbred and Cleveland Bay blood was introduced in order to produce horses suitable for both riding and carriage work. Since World War II, more Thoroughbred blood has been added.

Today, the Holstein is a first-class, all-round saddle horse, extensively used for show-jumping. It is also, with the revival of interest in driving, making a name for itself as a harness horse.

The Holstein is bred principally in the Elmshorn area of West Germany. Standing from 15.3 to 16.2 hh, the Holstein is powerfully built, with good shoulders, strong quarters, a good depth of girth, and short legs with plenty of bone. It is good-tempered, willing and intelligent, and its usual colours are bay, brown and black.

The Hanoverian makes an excellent dressage horse.

A Holstein ridden by ▶ the great German show-jumper Hans Winkler clears one of the fences during the 1976 Olympic Games at Montreal.

The Holstein

THE OLDENBURG

This breed is the heaviest of the German warm bloods. Its origins go back to the 17th century, when it was based on the Friesian Horse, and was originally developed to be a good, strong carriage horse. The first infusions of outside blood were Spanish and Eastern; later came Thoroughbred, Cleveland Bay, Anglo-Norman and Hanoverian. When the need for carriage horses dwindled in the early part of this century, more Thoroughbred blood was added, making the Oldenburg what could be called a half-bred saddle horse of heavy type.

As well as being the heaviest of the warm bloods, the Oldenburg is the tallest, standing from 16.2 to 17.2 hh. In spite of its height, it remains a compact horse, with short legs and plenty of bone. It has a deep girth and a notably strong back, and from its cold-blooded ancestors it inherits the useful quality of early maturity. It has a kind, yet bold, nature. The usual colours are bay, black, brown and grey.

Today, the wheel of fashion has turned full circle, and the Oldenburg is enjoying renewed popularity as a carriage horse, doing extremely well in competitive driving events.

Oldenburgers in a competitive team

THE WURTTEMBERG

The Wurttemberg goes back to the 16th century, when it was developed by putting local mares of varying type to Arab stallions. Later, East Prussian (Trakehner) blood was introduced, as well as Norman, Oldenburg and Nonius, producing a useful animal suitable for all-purpose work on the small farms of the Wurttemberg area. A Stud Book was started in 1895 when the type was considered established, largely owing to the influence of an Anglo-Norman stallion called *Faust.*

With the recent addition of more Trakehner blood, the Wurttemberg of today is a strong, cobby type, suitable for both riding and driving. In height, it averages 16 hh. It is a well-built horse, with good legs and feet and is a willing worker and economical feeder. The usual colours are bay, brown, black and chestnut.

The Wurttemberg makes a good heavyweight riding horse.

The Schleswig Heavy Draught Horse

THE SCHLESWIG HEAVY DRAUGHT HORSE

This breed claims a long ancestry, having been used in the Middle Ages as a saddle horse for heavily armoured knights. The province of Schleswig once belonged to Denmark, so it is not surprising that the breed was based on Danish Jutland horses. Later, Cleveland Bay and some Thoroughbred blood was introduced to provide a more active animal, suitable as an artillery horse as well as an agricultural worker. Since World War II, some Boulonnais and Breton blood has been added.

The Schleswig of today is a medium-sized, compact, cobby animal, and a willing worker, with a placid disposition. At one time, it was widely used for pulling buses and trams. It stands between 15.2 and 16 hh, and the predominant colour is chestnut, though there are some bays and greys.

THE RHINELAND HEAVY DRAUGHT HORSE

This breed takes its name from the Rhineland of Germany, where it was developed in the 19th century, when there was a great demand for draught horses. The Rhineland Heavy Draught has been much influenced by the Belgian Brabançon. It is a big, powerful horse, noted both for· its early maturity and for being an economical feeder.

Rhineland Heavy Draught horses add character to a German festival.

It stands from 16 to 17 hh, and is massively built, with strong shoulders and quarters, a deep, strong back, and short, strong legs. The neck is arched. Its characteristic colour is red-chestnut, with lighter mane and tail, but is also often red, or brown, roan. A good-tempered and willing worker, it is still bred in Saxony and Westphalia.

Switzerland
THE EINSIEDLER

At the abbey of Einsiedeln, near Zurich, horses have been bred continuously for a thousand years. The type has naturally undergone changes since Benedictine monks founded the abbey in 934. Horses then had to take the abbot and his retinue on religious journeys, work the abbey lands, and be of general use as transport. They were always good strong horses, and many went into Italy as mounts for the Italian cavaliers of the time, when they were known as the 'Horses of Our Lady'.

During the last century, several imported stallions had great influence on the breed, notably *Bracken,* from Yorkshire, which was probably a Cleveland Bay ; two Anglo-Normans, *Corail* and *Égalité;* and an English Hackney, *Thirtleby Saxonia.* The mare families at Einsiedeln today all trace back to one or other of those stallions. Stud Books were founded in 1840 and 1895.

An Einsiedler mare and foal in the grounds of the abbey at Einsiedeln.

The Franches-Montagnes

THE FRANCHES-MONTAGNES

The Einsiedler is a horse of medium height, standing from 15.1 to 16 hh, and is a clean-legged, deep-bodied animal with good shoulders, good bone and substance, free, level action and considerable quality. It is long-lived — the average age is 18 — and very hardy. The young horses spend their summers on high mountain pastures; in winter they are back at the abbey, but are out by day however deep the snow.

A very adaptable horse, the Einsiedler goes well in harness, can do light agricultural work, and is an excellent ride, capable of competitive dressage and show-jumping. Temperamentally, it is exceptionally kind, perhaps because through the long centuries of its existence, it has been looked after with sympathy and understanding. The usual colours are bay and chestnut, though any whole colour is permissible.

The Franches-Montagnes is a small draught horse that originated in the Jura region of Switzerland about a hundred years ago, when Anglo-Norman stallions were imported and crossed with local mares. In the early days of the breed, some Ardennais blood was also introduced. Since then, the breed has remained pure, and the type true and constant.

These horses, being small and particularly sure-footed, are eminently suitable for work on hill farms in mountainous districts and are still popular agricultural work-horses today. Their average height is around 15 hh, and in conformation they are stocky animals, with powerful bodies set on strong, short legs. Like most cobby types, they are active and willing. As they invariably have good temperaments, it is not surprising that even in this mechanical age, they continue to be widely used.

81

The Alter-Real

Portugal
THE ALTER-REAL

This breed has had a chequered history. Based on the Andalusian, it originated in the 18th century at the Vila de Portel Stud in Alentejo Province, which imported some 300 mares from the Jérez region of Spain. Because Alter-Reals proved excellent 'haute école' horses, the breed flourished and was in great demand. During the Napoleonic invasion, however, the stud was sacked and the horses dispersed; the remaining Alters were for many subsequent years crossed with a variety of breeds, from Arab to Hanoverian. It was not until the beginning of this century that steps were taken to re-introduce Andalusian blood and establish the old type again.

It says much for the Alter-Real that it has survived these vicissitudes, and is today a quality riding horse, with a marked ability for 'haute école'; although it has a highly strung temperament and needs to be handled with care.

It stands from 15.2 to 16 hh, and is a compact horse, with an elegant head and excellent conformation. Its action has great elevation. The Alter-Real is usually bay or brown, and occasionally grey.

THE LUSITANO

The Lusitano is similar to the Andalusian, from which it derives, together with infusions of different Eastern blood from time to time. It is a highly intelligent, agile horse of great courage. For these reasons it was in the past an excellent cavalry horse. Today, it is much used in the Portuguese bullring, where bull-fighting is carried on differently from in Spain.

Portuguese bullfighters, called *rejoneadores*, are mounted. As it is a disgrace to allow the horse to be touched by the bull, the rejoneador must be a highly skilled

A highly schooled Lusitano and its rejoneador rider in a bullring in Portugal.

horseman, and his Lusitano mount trained to a high standard: many 'haute école' movements are practical necessities. Unlike the sorry creatures used by some Spanish picadors, the rejoneador's horse is a prized and valuable animal.

The Lusitano stands from 15 to 16 hh. The head is small and well-modelled, set on to a fairly thick, arched neck. The shoulders are good, and the quarters powerfully muscled. The usual colour is grey, but can be bay, black or chestnut.

Spain
THE ANDALUSIAN

This famous breed dates back to the Moorish occupation of Spain, when Barb horses from North Africa were introduced into the country and crossed with existing Spanish stock. The result of this mingling of blood was a horse that for many centuries became the foremost riding horse of Europe, greatly influencing other European breeds, notably the Lipizzaner.

The breed owes much to the Carthusian monks of the 15th century, who devoted time, expertise and money to maintaining the purity of the Andalusian at their monasteries at Jérez, Seville and Cazallo. Originating in the Jérez region of Spain, the Andalusian is bred there to this day, principally at the Terry Stud.

Standing from 15.2 to 16 hh, the Andalusian is a horse of immense presence. The head, with its straight profile, is set on to a fairly thick neck; the shoulders are sloping; the body is elegantly proportioned; and the legs are strong and durable. The mane and tail are luxuriant. The action is spectacular and the bearing proud. The temperament is unusually docile for an animal of this quality. The usual colours are grey, brown, bay and black.

An Andalusian at the Terry Stud

THE SORRAIA PONY

The Sorraia Pony, mouse dun in colour.

This is Spain's only native pony. It comes from the western part of the country, bordering Portugal, from those regions watered by the Sorraia River and its tributaries. It is a true primitive type, having characteristics of both the Tarpan, and of Przewalski's Horse. It is usually yellow or golden dun in colour, with an eel stripe and zebra markings on the legs. The head is rather large, with a straight or sometimes convex profile; the ears are long, with black tips. The shoulder is fairly straight, while the quarters are under-developed, and the legs are long without a lot of bone.

Sorraia ponies are very hardy and are able to survive on poor pasture and to endure extremes of climate. In the past, they were used for agricultural work, but since mechanisation, their numbers have declined. The breed has also tended to degenerate, due to haphazard breeding resulting from many of the ponies running more or less wild. It would be a pity if the Sorraia were to become extinct. With the general increase of interest in ponies in Europe, it is probable that steps will be taken to resuscitate it and improve the stock. The Sorraia stands from 12.2 to 13 hh.

Italy

The Italian Heavy Draught Horse

THE ITALIAN HEAVY DRAUGHT HORSE

This very good-looking, medium-sized draught horse used to be a popular agricultural worker throughout central and northern Italy. It carries Breton blood, and like the Breton, is essentially a cobby type.

It stands from 15 to 16 hh, and has a good shoulder, a deep girth,

well-sprung ribs and rounded, muscular quarters. The neck is short and powerful, and the head very well modelled for a heavy horse. Its characteristic colour is a rich liver chestnut, with a flaxan mane and tail, though there are also some roans and ordinary chestnuts. Like most cobs, it is free, active and willing; but like so many heavy horses today, it is unfortunately bred mostly for meat.

Hungary

THE NONIUS

This breed originated and was developed at the Mezchegves Stud in Hungary. It takes its name from its foundation sire, *Nonius*, a French stallion foaled in 1810 after the mating of an English half-bred mare with a Norman stallion. During the Napoleonic wars, *Nonius* was captured by the Hungarians, and for them he sired 15 outstanding stallions from a variety of mares: Arabian, Holstein, Lipizzaner and Anglo-Norman. From *Nonius* and his 15 male offspring, the breed gradually became established, and is known today for producing good carriage and competitive riding horses.

Because of the variety of the type of the foundation mares, the Nonius can vary in height from 14.2 to 16 hh; but all are tough, compact horses of good bone and substance; up to a lot of weight for their height, with quality heads set on to well-arched necks. They have equable, sensible temperaments, and being late developers, can have longer than normal working lives. The usual colours are black, brown and bay.

A Nonius stallion

THE FURIOSO

This breed, like the Nonius, takes its name from one of its two foundation stallions: the English Thoroughbred *Furioso,* foaled in 1836. The other was the Norfolk Trotter *North Star,* foaled in 1844. Both these stallions were mated with local Nonius mares. Subsequent further infusions of Thoroughbred blood have produced a breed of quality horses, capable of competing at the highest level in all equestrian sports.

The average height of the Furioso is around 16 hh. The conformation is workmanlike, with strong jumping quarters, hocks well let-down, and strongly muscled thigh and second thigh. The usual colours are black and brown.

THE MURAKOZ

The Murakoz is a draught horse bred in the Mura district of Hungary, and also in Poland and Czechoslovakia. It has been developed this century by crossing native mares with Percheron, Ardennais and Noriker stallions, as well as with home-bred horses. The breed is now fixed, and in the early 1920s was so popular that it accounted for one-fifth of all the horses in Hungary. Unfortunately, it suffered heavy losses in World War II, and has not yet regained its former numbers.

The Murakoz stands, on average, 16 hh, and is a good-looking, fast-moving draught horse of quality. It has a well-modelled head and neat ears, powerful shoulders and quarters, and a well-sprung rib cage. It stands on short, strong legs which carry little feather. The Murakoz is known for being sound, tractable, an economical feeder and a good agricultural worker. The usual colour is liver chestnut, with a flaxen mane and tail, but black, grey, brown and bay do sometimes occur.

The Furioso

The Murakoz

Austria

THE HAFLINGER

The Haflinger is a hardy mountain pony originating in the Austrian Tyrol. It takes its name from the village of Hafling (which is now in Northern Italy), the centre of a district where the ponies were extensively bred. The breed traces back on one side to the Arabian, on the other to various cold-blood breeds. This combination makes the Haflinger ideal both for light draught work, and for riding. It is very sure-footed and has a charming temperament, making it an excellent pony for children and beginners. It is particularly suitable for pony-trekking.

Haflingers are widely bred throughout Austria, but private owners are allowed to keep only mares, and of course geldings. Stallions are all state-owned and kept at government stud farms. Colt foals have to undergo rigorous inspection, only a few being passed for use as stallions.

The Noriker

Today, the ponies are bred in some 20 other countries, including Germany, Switzerland, Holland, France, and Britain.

In height, the Haflinger should not exceed 14.2 hh; usually they are slightly smaller. Their conformation is sturdy, and they are unusually strong for their size. They have, however, a good neck giving a good length of rein. In colour, they are always chestnut, from light gold to rust, and the mane and tail are always flaxen.

THE NORIKER

This breed takes its name from the ancient state of Noricum, which corresponded roughly to what is now Austria. The Noriker is also called the German Cold Blood, and is bred throughout southern Germany as well as in Austria. The breed's original ancestors were probably Haflingers, but whereas the Haflinger is a pony, the Noriker is a horse, and owes its greater size to infusions of Spanish, Neapolitan and Burgundian blood. The term 'Noriker' now includes the Pinzgauer, a horse of similar type, but spotted, and which was formerly a separate breed.

Today, Norikers are widely used for agricultural work in the mountainous districts of Austria and southern Germany. They are sure-footed, active, light draught horses; and the breed is kept to a high standard by careful stallion selection. Colts have to undergo weight-pulling, walking and trotting trials before being allowed to be used as stallions.

In height, the Noriker stands between 16 and 16.2 hh. It has a fairly heavy head set on a short, thick neck. It is deep-chested, with a well-sprung rib cage, and has strong clean legs. It has an excellent temperament and is a willing worker. The usual colours are bay and chestnut.

A herd of Haflinger mares and foals graze peacefully at the Vanlay Stud in Austria.

Intelligence and beauty are combined in this fine Haflinger head, with its flaxen mane and forelock.

THE LIPIZZANER

This breed, renowned throughout the world for its association with the Spanish Riding School of Vienna, takes its name from the place where it was first bred, the stud at Lipizza, founded in 1580.

However, the breed originated earlier, in the 1560s, when horses subsequently known as Kladrubers were imported into Austria to pull the state coaches. These were big animals of mixed Andalusian and Neapolitan blood. The lighter, smaller and more elegant Lipizzaner was developed from crosses between Kladrubers, small horses from northern Italy, and Arabs.

The Spanish Riding School horses are bred at the famous Austrian Stud at Piber, which was started with six foundation stallions of different strains, each line being carried on distinctively. As well as being magnificent school horses, with an aptitude, probably by now hereditary, for 'haute école', Lipizzaners go well in harness, and make excellent private riding horses. They have great presence, are intelligent, and have ardent, yet docile, temperaments. They mature late, and are consequently long-lived, some working well into their twenties.

Standing on average around 15 hh, in conformation Lipizzaners combine power with grace. Their heads show their Arab ancestry: well-modelled, and wide between big, intelligent eyes. The neck and shoulders are strong, the back well ribbed up, the quarters muscular, and the legs strong with good bone. The usual colour is grey, though some families also produce browns and bays. Foals of grey parents are born black or brown, and turn grey as they mature.

Lipizzaner mares and foals at the Piber Stud, Austria.

The Kladruber

Czechoslovakia

THE KLADRUBER

Horses of mixed Andalusian and Neopolitan blood were first brought to Kladruby in the mid-16th century by the Emperor Maximilian II. In 1579, the Czech king and the Holy Roman Emperor combined to form Kladruby into a Royal Stud, for the purpose of breeding ceremonial coach horses, to be known as Kladrubers. In those days, odd colours were fashionable, and Kladrubers were often piebald, skewbald, dun, or even spotted. Later, when court ceremonial became more formal, grey and black were preferred, and since then these have been the two characteristic Kladruber colours. They are bred at separate State Studs: greys at Kladruby, blacks at Slatjiniany.

The Kladruby Stud, on the lower Elbe not far from Pardubice, has been in existence for nearly 400 years, with one break during the Seven Years' War. It was re-established in 1770 by the Emperor Franz Josef, and the breed, which had become somewhat inbred, improved through the importation of some Lipizzaner mares and horses of Spanish blood.

The Kladruber of today is smaller and more active than the original coach horse, which sometimes stood as high as 18 hh. Averaging around 16.2 hh, it is a horse with an impressive outlook and a strong, high-actioned trot. The head is well-modelled, with large, clear eyes, and the neck is powerful and crested. The withers are not pronounced, the neck flowing into an elegant top-line over a fairly light body. The tail is set high, the quarters strong, the cannon short with good bone. While still essentially a harness horse, the Kladruber is also used to produce good cross-bred riding horses, to which it passes on its equable temperament.

Poland

THE WIELKOPOLSKI

Two separate breeds have combined to form what is now known as the Wielkopolski: the Poznan and the Masuren. The Poznan contained Arab, Thoroughbred and Hanoverian blood, while the Masuren was based on the Trakehner. The Wielkopolski of today has therefore been developed from these four main blood lines, and is bred mainly at the State Stud at Racot.

There are, however, regional variations of type in the animals bred in other districts. And while the term 'Wielkopolski' designates a specific breed, it is also used to cover all Polish warm-blood horses, and can

include a recently developed breed, the Malapolski. This is similar, but lighter, and is bred in south-west Poland.

The Wielkopolski is around 16 hh in height, and is of good conformation, showing many of the best characteristics of the excellent breeds that have contributed to it. It has a quality head, set on to a lean, well-shaped neck; good shoulders and withers; a deep girth; well-muscled quarters and strong legs with short cannon and good bone, making it up to weight as a riding horse. The Wielkopolski is of sound constitution, has a good temperament, and is a notably good mover. It can be of any whole colour.

THE KONIK

The Konik is similar to the Hucul, being also descended from the Tarpan, but it has had rather more infusions of Arab blood and has developed a more quality outline. It is used on lowland farms in Poland and other parts of eastern Europe, to which it has been exported. It is selectively bred at two State Studs, at Popielmo and Jezewice, as well as by many small farmers for their own use. A little bigger than the Hucul, its average height is 13.1 hh. It is also tough and hardy, a willing worker and an economical feeder. It is always dun in colour.

The Konik

THE HUCUL PONY

The Hucul is one of the few breeds of native pony still existing on the continent of Europe, and is one of the oldest. Native to the Carpathians, where herds have wandered for thousands of years, it is probably a direct descendant of the Tarpan, which it resembles more than any other native pony. Recently, some Arab blood has been introduced to improve the breed, which is being selectively bred at several studs, mainly at Siary, near Gorlice.

The Hucul is very hardy, makes an excellent pack and draught pony, and is widely used on hill farms. In height, it ranges from 12.1 to 13 hh. It has the characteristic primitive short head, a rather poor back and a low-set tail. It is sure-footed, strong and willing, and its predominant colours are dun and bay.

Hucul ponies

Soviet Union
THE AKHAL-TEKÉ

This is one of the oldest and most beautiful breeds in existence, being a strain of the ancient Turkoman horse which was the favoured mount of Eastern warriors 2500 years ago. Akhal-Tekés were developed by the Teké, or Turkoman tribe in the oases of Turkmenistan. They were traditionally kept covered in blankets and fed an unusual diet of barley, lucerne and even mutton fat.

Because of the arid conditions in which they were bred, the horses developed great endurance and can work in conditions of extreme heat and cold. In 1935 Akhal-Tekés took part in a famous long trek from Ashkhabad to Moscow, a distance of over 2500 miles (4000 km). On the journey these remarkable horses crossed 235 miles (376 km) of desert in three days without water.

The average height of Akhal-Tekés is from 14.2 to 15.2 hh, and their conformation is distinctive and elegant. They have fine Eastern heads, with large expressive eyes; long, lean necks and bodies, with sloping quarters; and the best of feet and legs. The mane and tail hair is sparse and silky. In their fine-drawn outline built for speed, they could be likened to the greyhound. They are specialised saddle horses. Although there are some bays and greys, the predominant and most desired colour is a pale honey-gold, with a metallic sheen.

The Akhal-Teké

THE DON

Since the 18th century, Don horses have been the mounts of the Don Cossacks. With them, the Cossacks harassed Napoleon's ill-fated army in 1812, marching to Paris, and back again across Europe into Russia — an unrivalled feat in cavalry history. The breed contains the blood of Turkomene and Karabakh stallions, which in the past were turned loose on the steppes to mate with the native mares. In the 19th century, some Thoroughbred and Arab blood was introduced, but since then there have been no outside influences.

Living for centuries on the steppes and having to forage for food in the harsh winters have made the Don an exceptionally tough horse, able to look after itself with the minimum of help from humans. Today, many still live and breed on the steppes and plains, ensuring that the breed retains the hardiness that is one of its basic characteristics.

The Don is a saddle horse of good repute, and is also driven. Standing between 15.1 and 15.3 hh, it is a strong, wiry animal, somewhat 'on the leg', but with a fine Eastern head. In conformation, it shows something of the lean, elegant outline inherited from its Eastern forebears, from which some also inherit the metallic, golden coat colour. The more usual colours are chestnut, bay and grey.

The Budyonny

THE BUDYONNY

The Budyonny takes its name from a Russian cavalry officer, Marshal Budyonny. He developed the breed in the early years of this century at the military stud at Rostov. The horse was intended for use by the Russian cavalry.

The breeding programme was to mate Don mares with Thoroughbred stallions, interbreeding the best of the progeny. The result is an excellent riding horse of quality, with a sensible temperament, and great stamina. It is versatile and speedy and is used today both for competitive equestrian sports and for steeplechasing.

In height, Budyonnys stand between 15.2 and 16 hh, and have good conformation, being deep-bodied, with good shoulders and quarters, strong legs with plenty of bone, and attractive heads set on lean, well-shaped necks. The predominant colour is chestnut, sometimes with a gold sheen, but there are also many bays and greys.

THE KABARDIN

This breed of small mountain h originated in the Caucasus some years ago, when Arab, Turkom and Karabakh stallions were run the native Mongolian mares. Kabardin is strong, sure-footed intelligent. It has a markedly veloped homing instinct, which i its advantage in negotiating tortuous mountain paths of its na land. It is exceptionally hardy, the stamina to undertake long j neys, and is used locally as a sp horse and for racing.

The Kabardin stands between and 15 hh. It has strong legs and g feet, and a better front than quar The usual colours are black and b

Two Kabardin horses

THE KARABAIR

The Karabair comes from Uzbekistan in Central Asia, a region renowned for more than 2000 years for the quality of its horses. The origins of the breed are lost in time, but are probably a mixture of Mongol and Arab blood. The Karabair is an excellent type of horse: spirited and with boundless endurance, yet tractable. It is the ideal mount for various Russian mounted games, including one in which the stuffed carcase of a goat has to be carried through goal posts.

The Karabair stands around 15 hh, and in conformation is rather like a stocky Arabian, with less refinement. The usual colours are bay, chestnut and grey.

The Karabair

THE ORLOV TROTTER

The Orlov Horse is named after its founder, Count Alexis Orlov, who developed the breed at his Khrenov Stud in 1777. He produced the Orlov Horse by crossing Arab, Thoroughbred, Friesian, Danish and Mecklenburg blood. The first stallion was an Arab called *Smetanka*, which, put to a Friesian mare, produced the stallion *Polkan*. The first official trotter was *Bars First*, a son of *Polkan* out of a black Friesian mare, which is considered the foundation stallion of the breed. Trotting races were held in Moscow as far back as 1799. As the sport prospered and became widely popular, so did the Orlov Trotter. Before the development of the American Standardbred, the Orlov was undoubtedly the best trotting horse in the world

An Orlov Trotter in action in races at Moscow.

he Orlov Trotter stands from 15.2
7 hh, and is a strong horse, with
/erful, if somewhat straight,
ulders; a fairly long back, but
1 plenty of depth through the
1; and strong, durable legs. It is a
gh, long-lived animal, and though
1 primarily for racing, it is also used
er saddle. The chief colours
grey and black.

recent years, with the introduc-
of imported Standard-bred blood,
Metis Trotter has been developed
the Orlov, the result being a
se that is faster, but not quite so
active as its progenitor.

An alert and intelligent Karabakh

THE KARABAKH

This very old and beautiful breed
belongs to the Caucasus, and probably, like the Akhal-Teké, traces back
to the ancient Persian Turkomene
horse, although it obviously has Arab
ancestry as well. It has the typical
Arabian dished profile, as opposed to
the straight profile of the Persian,
and it is not so fine-drawn and
greyhound-like in outline as the
Akhal-Teké. Karabakh stallions have
in the past contributed much to the
improvement of the Don breed.

Standing from just under 15 to 16
hh, the Karabakh is a well-proportioned horse, with admirable
conformation. The fine, Arab-type
head is set on to a well-formed,
slightly arched neck. The shoulders
are good, the hocks well let-down,
and in contrast to the lean lines of the
Akhal-Teké, the body is compact and
deep. The Karabakh is also of a
calmer temperament. It does, however, share with the Akhal-Teké its
characteristic coat colour — a pale
honey-gold with a metallic sheen.

THE RUSSIAN HEAVY DRAUGHT HORSE

The Russian Heavy Draught Horse

Although a heavy draught horse in the sense of being powerful and fit for heavy work, the Russian Heavy Draught is in fact a relatively small animal. It is of cobby type, similar to that of several of the French draught horse breeds, one of which, the Ardennais, has contributed to its make-up.

The Russian Heavy Draught Horse has been developed during the last 100 years, principally in the Ukraine. Ardennais, Percheron and Orlov stallions were used on local draught-type mares, the best of the progeny being then inter-bred to produce a fixed type. The infusion of Orlov blood is probably what has given this sturdy little horse rather more presence than is often found in draught animals.

In height, the Russian Heavy Draught stands only around 14.2 hh. It is an active, willing and kind horse, noted for its great pulling power. In conformation, it is compact, with strong shoulders and quarters, a well-sprung rib cage and fairly short, strong legs carrying some feather.

The Russian Heavy Draught is widely used on the farms of the Ukraine and in the Urals. Because of its smaller size, it is a more economical horse to keep than some of the bigger, heavier draught breeds.

THE VLADIMIR HEAVY DRAUGHT HORSE

The Vladimir Heavy Draught Horse

This very powerful draught horse originated in 1886, when a variety of light and heavy draught horses were imported to the stables at Gavrilovo-Posadsk for crossing with local mares. From England came Suffolk Punches and Cleveland Bays; from France, Percherons and Ardennais. Later, at the beginning of this century, Clydesdale and Shire blood was introduced, the Shire predominating. From 1925 onwards no more outside blood was introduced, the policy being to interbreed the best of the progeny, and by 1950 the breed was considered to be fixed. Vladimirs are today bred in the Ivanovo and Vladimir regions.

The Vladimir of today closely resembles the Shire, which would seem to have had the greatest influence in forming the breed, although the Vladimir is smaller, standing usually around 16 hh. It is a strong, well-built horse, with good free action, deriving perhaps from the Clydesdale.

It also has sound limbs carrying plenty of feather. Like most heavy horses, it has a kind and tractable temperament. It is used for heavy draught work, and on the land. All whole colours are permissible, and white markings on the head and legs are prevalent.

THE VIATKA PONY

The Viatka stems from the Klepper, a branch of the great and varied family of ponies native to northern Europe; it belongs to the Northern Forest group, all of which are particularly hardy. Bred chiefly in the basins of the Viatka and Obva rivers, the ponies are used for light agricultural work, for riding, and, because they are very speedy, for pulling *troika* sledges. In winter, they grow very thick coats, and carry a layer of fat under the skin to protect them from the cold.

The Viatka stands between 13 and 14 hh. It has a small head with a concave profile that shows some quality, though the lower jaw is often rather thick. The neck is strong, the shoulders and quarters well-muscled, the girth deep, the legs strong and short, and the feet hard. The mane and tail are luxuriant. The characteristic colours of the Viatka are those of many native north European ponies: shades of dun, with an eel stripe, and often zebra markings on the legs. Bay and roan are also sometimes seen. A very active pony, the Viatka is a good doer and therefore economical to keep.

The Viatka Pony

An exciting ride on a Lokai Pony

THE LOKAI

The Lokai is a hardy mountain horse from the Uzbekistan and Tadzhik-stan regions of the Soviet Union. It was developed from Mongol horses in the 16th century by the Lokai people of the area. The breed was later improved with Iomud, Karabair and Arab blood. Its easy and willing temperament makes the Lokai suitable not only for riding and carrying loads but also for sport, in which it displays great agility and courage. It is used for racing, hunting, hawking and the local sport of *kop-kopi*, in which galloping riders try to snatch a goat carcase from each other.

The Lokai stands up to 14.2 hh in height. Its head is short, with a straight or convex profile. The neck is straight, and the body close-coupled, with sloping quarters and croup. The legs are strong, with good bone, but there is a tendency to sickle hocks.

In colour, the Lokai is generally bay, sometimes grey or chestnut or, more rarely, black or dun.

Asia

THE MANIPURI

The Manipuri can claim to be the original polo pony. Ancient manuscripts prove that the reigning King of Manipur introduced the game in the 7th century, using ponies bred in his State. It was probably on this pony that the British in India discovered polo, before taking the game to Europe and then to the Americas.

The Manipuri had also been used for war and was the mount of the formidable Manipur cavalry which, in the 17th century, was feared throughout Upper Burma. As recently as World War II, Manipuris were the valued transport ponies that accompanied the British 14th Army into Burma in 1945.

Descended from the Mongolian Wild Horse and from the Arab, the Manipuri, although seldom exceeding

An old photograph of a Manipuri Pony and rider

13.2 hh, is strong, fast and intelligent, and has great stamina. In conformation, the head, set on to a clean, muscular neck, is fairly long, with an alert, gentle outlook; the muzzle is broad and the nostrils well dilated. The chest is broad, the body compact, with well-sprung ribs. The shoulder is good, and the quarters well developed. The legs are in proportion, and are clean and durable, with strong knees and hocks. The Manipuri can be any colour.

Until the recent fashion of playing big animals, the Manipuri was probably the ideal polo pony, for the game calls for speed, agility, strength and intelligence.

THE KATHIAWARI AND THE MARWARI

The Kathiawari and the Marwari are more or less identical, the two names having arisen from the two districts, Kathiawar and Marwar, of which they are natives. Traditionally they are said to be descended from a ship-load of Arab horses that was wrecked off the west coast of India. These ran wild and inter-bred with the indigenous country-bred ponies. Certainly their inward-pointing ears, almost meeting at the tips, indicate Arab ancestry; as does, unfortunately, their tendency to sickle hocks.

In height, the ponies range from 14 to 15 hh, and in conformation, they are light and narrow, with rather poor necks and quarters. Like all countrybreds, however, they are tough, hardy, economical feeders, and possessed of stamina. They have comfortable, easy paces, but rather uncertain tempers. The best are used for racing, and in the days of the height limit, were also used for polo. In Marwar, which in the Middle Ages was a great horse-breeding district, they have also been prominent as war-horses.

There are several studs of these

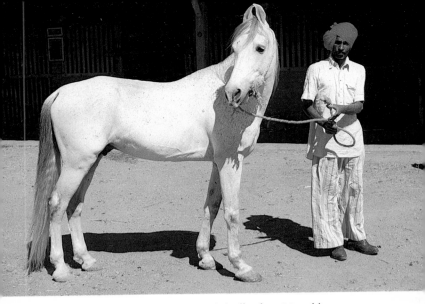

A Kathiawari demonstrating the characteristically almost touching ears.

ponies, which are eminently suitable both to the wild nature of the country to which they belong, and to the needs of its inhabitants. They can be any colour, including piebald and skewbald.

THE TIMOR PONY

Native to the island of Timor, this is the smallest of the Indonesian ponies, and is used by the people as a cow-pony. It is also imported into Australia and New Zealand, where it is of good repute as a child's pony. In Australia, the breed has been used, together with Thoroughbred, Arab and imported Welsh Mountain and Shetland, to create a type of Australian Riding Pony.

The Timor Pony stands only from 11 to 12 hh, but is exceptionally strong for its size. It possesses great stamina, and although fast, active and willing, it is temperamentally docile and sensible: inestimable qualities in a child's pony. It has good conformation: a neat pony head; a well-proportioned and well set-on neck; a short strong back, and good shoulders and hind legs. The usual colours are bay, black and brown, but there are also some unusual ones: a dark chocolate brown, with cream mane and tail, being particularly attractive.

The Timor Pony

THE CASPIAN PONY

These remarkable little animals are more like tiny horses than ponies. They were thought to have become extinct, until in 1965 a number were found running wild on the shores of the Caspian Sea. Some were also discovered pulling carts in the coastal towns of northern Iran. They are obviously a true breed, and while it is not yet possible to be certain of their origin, the prevalent theory is that they are the lineal descendants of the Miniature Horse of Mesopotamia, known to have existed there from about 3000 BC until the 7th century AD. What then became of them, and how they survived, are still uncertain.

Standing from only 10 up to 12.2 hh, the Caspian is intelligent, easily handled, sure-footed, and a natural jumper. Being also narrow, it is an excellent mount for small children. In conformation, it is a truly miniature horse, being relatively longer on the leg than a pony, with the cannon longer, and the bone, though hard, lighter. The Caspian is clean-legged. The head is fine and of Arab type; the eyes are large and set wide apart. The colour is bay or brown, with no white markings.

The Caspian is really a miniature horse.

Africa
THE BASUTO PONY

The Basuto Pony is not indigenous to southern Africa. Horses were unknown there until 1653, when four animals of Arabian and Barb blood were brought to the Cape area by the Dutch East India Company. These were the founders of what became known as the Cape Horse. Over the years, additions of further Oriental and English Thoroughbred blood helped to establish the breed. Among the horses imported by the English settlers were descendants of such horses as *Herod, Matchem* and *Eclipse*. The Cape Horse, therefore, was a hot blood of distinguished ancestry.

In the early 19th century, as a result of skirmishes between Zulus and settlers, Cape horses were taken as spoils of war to Basutoland (now Lesotho). There, harsh conditions in the Drakensberg and inter-breeding with local horses caused them to lose height and degenerate in type. But as time passed, they developed into the strong, hardy and sure-footed animals known today as the Basuto Pony.

Standing only up to 14.2 hh, Basutos have great stamina as well as strength; many have carried full-grown men up to 80 miles (128 km) in a day. For a time, the breed declined both in numbers and quality. However, its pas reputation is so high that, hopefully, contemporary selective breeding and the re-introduction of some Arabian blood will preserve its original character: that of a thick-set, sturdy, versatile pony with short strong legs, a longish back, a graceful neck and a quality head denoting its high ancestry. The usual colours are bay, chestnut, brown and grey.

A Basuto Pony at a village in Lesotho

A mouse dun Cutting Horse

Canada

THE CANADIAN CUTTING HORSE

The Cutting Horse is the Canadian equivalent of the American Quarter Horse, from which the breed largely derives. The term 'cutting' refers to the work principally required of it: the 'cutting out', or separating, of a particular animal from a herd or mob of cattle. This calls for great skill, on the part of the horse as well as the rider. A good cutting horse will seem to know its job so well that it appears to be doing it on its own; turning and twisting to single out the chosen beast, often leaning its full weight against it at what seem impossible angles, and usually at high speed.

Canadian Cutting Horses are highly intelligent, and seem to have an innate talent for this work. They are therefore bred mainly to compete in the many cutting competitions held throughout the year, the best horses winning their riders large sums.

Standing on average around 15.2 hh, the Cutting Horse is similar in conformation to the American Quarter Horse, with a strong, short back, and muscular thigh and second thigh. It is also used for Western and for pleasure riding. It can be of almost any colour.

110

Australia
THE WALER

The first horses arrived in Australia 1788, brought by Governor Art Phillip who, stopping at the Cape Good Hope for supplies, took board six Cape horses: a stalli three mares and two fillies. arrival, all but the stallion and mare unfortunately escaped fr their grooms and disappeared into the bush. However, more horses were imported during the next ten years — horses from the Cape, and Thoroughbreds and Arabs. By 1798, Australia had 117 horses of mixed origin.

Thereafter, numbers increased rapidly. Their quality was improved by the importation of selected stallions, an English horse named *Rockingham* being particularly influential. By the early 1820s, there were over 5,000 domesticated horses in Australia; they were called 'Walers' after the first settlement, the State of New South Wales. These Walers were — and still are — strong, hardy animals of dense bone, capable of carrying 17 stone (108 kg) on a day's work. They were in great demand as army remounts. During the Boer War, over 16,000 served as cavalry horses; in World War I, over 121,000.

In Australia, the Waler was indispensable to the early settlers. A tough, courageous horse endowed with speed, stamina and considerable quality, it is used today as a stock horse and a police horse. It would be a pity if the contemporary emphasis on bloodstock breeding were to lead to the decline of the Waler, whose contribution to the development of Australia has been inestimable. In height, the Waler averages around 16 hh, and can be any whole colour.

The Australian Waler

United States
THE AMERICAN SADDLE HORSE

The American Saddle Horse, showing the distinctive tail setting.

The official founder of the American Saddle Horse is the Thoroughbred stallion *Denmark*, foaled in 1839. The origin of the breed, however, goes back much further, to the days when the pioneers needed strong, hardy, speedy, light horses that were comfortable to ride for long distances, good-tempered and intelligent, and capable of going in harness. Since there were no indigenous horses in America, the pioneers had to breed selectively from stock brought with them, or imported soon after: English amblers and pacers (which came before the Thoroughbred), and horses from Spain, France, Africa and the East. The blood of all these went to make what was first called the Kentucky Saddle Horse. Since the days of *Denmark,* Morgan and American Standardbred blood has been introduced.

Today, the American Saddle Horse is bred primarily for the show-ring, where it can compete in three classes: light harness, three-gaited, and five-gaited. The five-gaited saddler is the most prized; it can perform two additional gaits to the normal walk, trot and canter. These are the *slow gait* and the *rack,* which are specialities of the breed. The slow gait is a prancing movement carried out in four time; the rack is its full-speed equivalent. Both show to advantage the breed's extravagant and elevated action.

The Saddle Horse stands between 15 and 16 hh, and in conformation should be light and elegant, with a small quality head set on a long fine neck, strong shoulders, back and quarters, and strong legs. The usual colours are bay, brown, chestnut and black.

The showy appearance of the Saddle Horse is accentuated by the artificially produced high tail carriage: the dock muscles are nicked and the tail set in a crupper. The extravagant action is encouraged by growing the feet long and fastening weights round the coronet.

THE TENNESSEE WALKING HORSE

The foundation sire of this popular breed was a Standardbred called *Black Allan*, foaled in 1886. It had a curious preference for travelling at a four-beat pace, which was half walk, half run, and this has become the characteristic pace of the Walking Horse. It is an extremely comfortable pace for the rider; many claim that the Tennessee Walking Horse is the most comfortable ride in the world.

Morgan and Naragansett Pacer blood have also gone to the making of the breed, which was developed originally by Southern plantation owners to carry them on their tours of inspection. They used to call this breed of horse the 'Turn Row', because of its ability to travel between the rows of crops without damaging them.

The Tennessee Walking Horse stands from 15 to 15.2 hh, and is of excellent conformation, with particularly powerful shoulders and hard, strong legs. It is intelligent and notably good-tempered, and the usual colours are black, bay and chestnut.

The Tennessee Walking Horse

THE STANDARDBRED

The Standardbred is probably the world's finest harness racehorse. Its official foundation sire was the English Thoroughbred, *Messenger*, which was imported into America in 1788, and which traced back in the male line to the Darley Arabian. Crossed with Naragansett Pacer mares, which were horses of Friesian origin imported by the early settlers, *Messenger's* progeny all showed marked trotting ability.

The prepotent *Hambletonian,* foaled in 1849, was one of *Messenger's* descendants, and is responsible for his being named the founder of the breed. Although some other Thoroughbred strains, and some Morgan and Norfolk Trotter blood, were introduced, 99 per cent of Standardbreds today trace to one or other of four of *Hambletonian's* sons: *George Wilkes, Dictator, Happy Medium,* and *Electioneer.*

The name 'Standardbred' dates

A Standardbred pacing

officially from 1879, when the National Association of Trotting Horse Breeders adopted a set of rules for admission into the Trotting Register based on a horse's attaining a se standard of speed. Originally a composite type, the Standardbred of today is a homogenous and firmly established breed, renowned the world over. All European trotting horses owe something to the Standardbred, which is also bred in Puerto Rico and New Zealand.

The Standardbred is a medium sized horse, standing from 15.2 to 16 hh. In conformation it has many Thoroughbred characteristics; but is more robustly built, with great depth of girth; powerful quarters, and short, strong, durable legs. It is a tremendously tough and courageous horse, with unequalled heart and stamina, which enable it to run heat after heat without flagging. Some Standardbreds both trot and pace; those with a natural tendency to pace are trained in this gait from an early age. In colour, Standardbreds are usually bay, brown, black or chestnut

THE MORGAN

This is the only breed which can truly be said to have sprung from one founding stallion, the little bay horse *Justin Morgan,* foaled in 1793 in Vermont. His ancestry is not precisely known, but he is thought to have been of mixed Thoroughbred and Arabian blood, with possibly also some Welsh. He was named after his second owner, Thomas Justin Morgan, who was so impressed by the horse's versatility, strength, endurance and good looks that he fortunately decided to try him at stud before having him gelded.

The results were astonishing. From varied, and often very ordinary mares, his progeny were almost all exact replicas of himself. As his fame grew, mares were sent to him from all over the country. Eventually he was bought for a large sum by the U.S. Army, who set up a Morgan Stud Farm in Woodstock, Vermont. So the little horse remained at stud for the rest of his life, establishing a breed almost unique in its trueness to original type. What is more, he stamped his stock so strongly that his own type was reproduced from generation to generation.

Justin Morgan died in 1821, but the breed he founded is still today one of the most popular of American pleasure horses. It has left its mark on many others, notably the Saddle and Tennessee Walking horses.

Justin Morgan himself stood only about 14 hh; the Morgan today can measure up to 15.1 or 15.2. But in conformation it retains his characteristics: compact, solidly built, muscular, with powerful shoulders, shapely legs and feet, and an attractive head set on a muscular, crested neck. The Morgan is an active, versatile horse, with boundless stamina and a kindly nature. The usual colours are bay, brown, chestnut and black.

THE QUARTER HORSE

This breed was developed by the early English colonists in Virginia and North and South Carolina, and is the result of crossing imported English stallions, mostly Thoroughbred, with resident mares of Spanish descent. They were used as all-round ride-and-drive horses, the name coming from the quarter-mile sprint races at which they were adept; these were races run on improvised tracks or along the main streets of villages.

When Thoroughbred racing became established, the unofficial sprints lapsed, but the Quarter Horse, having proved itself an admirable cow-pony kept its popularity. Over the years it has developed a remarkable instinct for herding and 'cutting out', or separating, cattle. It is an attractive, good-natured, versatile and intelligent horse of great agility, and is today one of America's most popular breeds being widely used as a pleasure horse. It is also exported to and bred in many other countries.

The Quarter Horse is of medium height, averaging around 15.2 hh and is of excellent conformation compact, with a short, strong, muscular back and particularly powerful quarters. It may be of any whole colour, but chestnut predominates.

The Quarter Horse, showing the powerful quarters that give it its strength and agility.

A Quarter Horse at work during a rodeo in the American West.

A Palomino mare and her foal take a drink at a water trough. Palomino foals darken in colour with age.

A fine Palomino stallion

THE PALOMINO

Until fairly recently, 'Palomino' simply meant an animal of a particular coat colour. Now, however, Palomino Breed Societies have been formed in America and Great Britain; and while correct coat colour is still essential for acceptance into their registers, conformation plays an equally important part. As a result, the standard of Palominos, both horses and ponies, has improved enormously. Palomino colouring, to be correct, should be that of a 'newly minted gold coin', or three shades lighter or darker; the mane and tail should be creamy white. White markings on the face and legs are allowed.

While breeding for good conformation is not so very difficult, breeding for correct colour is, and is still largely a hit or miss affair. The crosses most likely to produce Palomino are: Palomino to Palomino; chestnut (with two chestnut parents) to Palomino; and chestnut or Palomino to albino. Foals tend to darken with age, and the coat colour is not considered to be 'set' until the animal is six years old.

Palominos can vary both in height and type from horses to quite small ponies; but thanks to the efforts of the Breed Societies, all registered Palominos are now animals of good conformation. The colour is said to have originated in Spain, where such horses were called *Isabellas*, after the queen of the period (1474-1504), but golden-coloured horses certainly existed long before then.

117

THE APPALOOSA

Appaloosas were originally bred by the Palouse and Nez Percé Indians, who lived in north-west America until 1877. They descended from horses taken to North America in the 16th century by the Spanish Conquistadores. For their distinctive markings to have come down through so many generations, there must have been a number of prepotent stallions with spotted coats among them.

The three main spot patterns are: an all-over pattern of dark spots on a white background, called *leopard;* light spots on a dark background, known as *snowflake;* and spots on the quarters and loins only, referred to as *spotted blanket*. Additional variations are *marble, frost* and *white blanket,* which is not really spotted but is a blanket of white over the quarters and loins on an otherwise dark coat. Apart from the leopard pattern, the usual basic coat colour is roan, though any colour is permissible that has one of the six basic spot patterns.

The skin of the nose, lips and genitals of Appaloosas is mottled, and there is often white sclera round the eyes. The mane and tail hair is sparse, and the hooves are sometimes vertically striped. With an average height around 15.2 hh, the Appaloosa is a compact horse, with powerful quarters. It is active, agile, of tractable temperament, possesses both speed and stamina, and is often an excellent jumper. The Appaloosa is a popular saddle horse in America today and is also used as a circus or a parade horse.

The Appaloosa, with its characteristics spots.

The Pinto, with its distinctive markings.

THE PINTO

The Pinto takes its name from the Spanish word meaning 'painted', and although originally a colour type only, it is now recognised in America as a breed. There are two coat colourings: *piebald*, which is black and white, and *skewbald*, which is any other colour or colours and white.

Within those colourings are two distinct patterns: the *Overo* and the *Tobiano*. In the Overo, the white markings start from the belly and extend upwards; the mane and tail are usually dark, and dark and white alternate on the legs, which are seldom all white. White faces and blue (glass) eyes are prevalent. In the Tobiano, the patches have no definite starting point; white legs are more usual, but white faces and blue eyes are infrequent. Tobianos tend to be bigger and heavier than Overos.

The Pinto was a favourite horse of the American Indian, its broken coat colour acting as camouflage. Today, as well as being frequently used in Wild West movies, the Pinto is a popular riding horse in America. There are also special classes for it at shows, where the accepted judging rule is 50 per cent for markings, and 50 per cent for conformation. There is no definite height ruling or conformation specification for Pintos, as breeding is concentrated on producing the right colouring.

THE PONY OF THE AMERICAS

This breed has only been in existence for 20 years, and was founded in a novel manner, by crossing a Shetland stallion with an Appaloosa mare. The Appaloosa markings are dominant; for registration, a pony must carry one of the accepted Appaloosa coat patterns. The idea was to produce a small, active child's pony, which would be versatile and easy to manage, and have plenty of substance. The breed has fulfilled these qualifications remarkably well. The ponies compete successfully in jumping classes; are used for trial rides, and make excellent, friendly, all-purpose children's mounts.

The Pony of the Americas

In height, the Pony of the Americas ranges from 11.2 to 13 hh. The head should be small and Arab-like, with a dished profile; the eyes should be large and the ears small. The shoulder should be sloping, the body deep, the quarters well rounded and the tail set high. The legs are short, with plenty of bone. The ponies are eye-catching animals, with straight, free action, and a kind, willing temperament.

Puerto Rico
THE PASO FINO

An old breed, descended from Spanish stock, the Paso Fino has a natural four-beat gait, probably inherited from the Spanish Jennet. Selective breeding has perpetuated its three distinctive paces, which are: the *paso fino*, slow and collected; the *paso corto*, faster and used for long-distance riding; and the *paso largo*, extended and fast, at which pace the horses can travel up to 16 miles an hour (25 kph). None of these paces has to be taught, and all are very comfortable for the rider.

The Paso Fino is a small animal, never more than 15 hh and often considerably less. It is of pony, rather than horse, type and character. It is sturdily built, with a neat, quality head and strong shoulders. It is intelligent, of good temperament, and can be any whole colour: Palominos are not unknown. The Paso Fino is also bred in Peru and Colombia.

Below: the Paso Fino from Puerto Rico.

Peru
THE PERUVIAN STEPPING HORSE

Although it is sometimes as small as the Paso Fino, the Peruvian Stepping Horse is definitely a small horse, not a pony. Descended also from Spanish stock, it too has a characteristic gait, which has been systematically developed. It is different from that of the Paso Fino and could be described as an 'amble': a kind of lateral trot, which the Stepping Horse performs with extravagant action of the forelegs, the hindlegs being powerfully driven forward with the quarters lowered. At this gait it can travel at up to 11 miles an hour (17 kph) over the roughest ground, and being possessed of great stamina, it can maintain this speed for long distances.

In height, the Stepping Horse ranges from 14 to 15.2 hh, and is a showy, well-made little horse with a lot of presence. The fine, quality head is set on a strong, arched neck; the girth is deep, the body close-coupled and the quarters muscular. The usual colours are chestnut and bay.

Below right: the Peruvian Stepping Horse.

Argentina

THE FALABELLA

The Falabella is the smallest horse in the world, standing at under 7 hh. It takes its name from the Falabella family, who created the breed on their ranch near Buenos Aires. This they did by crossing small Thoroughbreds with small Shetlands, and then inter-breeding. The Falabella's principal purpose is as a pet, since it is very friendly and intelligent. It is not suitable for riding, but is sometimes used in harness.

The Falabella could be regarded as a family pet.

THE CRIOLLO

If any horse can be called native to South America, it is the Criollo. It is, however, descended from Spanish stock (Andalusian, Arab and Barb). When Indians sacked Buenos Aires, the Spaniards' horses were driven out on to the pampas, and for 300 years ran wild. In the struggle for survival, they suffered rigorous natural selection; the weak and unsound perished, and only the best physical specimens survived the hazards of fires, floods, frosts, great changes of temperature and attacks by wild dogs. It is not surprising that the Criollo has developed into an outstandingly tough, stalwart, active and resourceful animal.

Criollos are used mainly as stock horses by the gauchos, and for general riding. They are horses of great endurance. It was two Criollos, *Mancha* and *Gato*, aged 15 and 16, which carried Professor Tschiffely on his remarkable ride from Buenos Aires to New York, a distance of 13,350 miles (21,485 km), averaging 26 miles (42 km) a day and achieving the altitude record of 19,250 feet (5867 metres).

Criollos stand from 13.3 to 14.3 hh, and are strong, compact, muscular animals, up to considerable weight.

The Criollo

The head is short and broad, the eyes wide-set. The neck and quarters are well developed, the chest wide, the withers well defined, and the back short and deep. The legs are muscular, the cannon bone short, with the tendons well separated, and the feet hard. In temperament, Criollos are bright, active and willing. Their predominant colour is dun. They are now bred in many South American countries.

GLOSSARY

Bone Apart from the everyday anatomical meaning, *bone* refers specifically to the measurement around a horse's cannon bone just below the knee. A horse with *good bone* has a measurement of between 8½ and 9½ inches (21-24 cm) and is capable of carrying more weight than one that is *light of bone*, whose measurement is less. Many native ponies can carry quite heavy weights because their bone can measure as much as that of many horses.

Clean-legged Describes a horse with no feather.

Close-coupled Compact in body, without too large a gap between the end of the rib cage and the quarters.

Cob A horse or pony with a particular kind of conformation: a well-rounded rib cage, a compact body, well-rounded and muscular quarters, relatively short legs with good bone and therefore strong and up to weight.

Cobby A *cobby type* is a horse or pony of any breed with the conformation characteristics of a cob.

Deep through the girth A good conformation feature, indicating a generous measurement around the barrel just behind the withers; this gives plenty of room for expansion of the lungs.

Dished Concave, referring to the profile of the head, such as that of the Arab.

Feather The hair on the back of the cannon bones and around the fetlocks.

Good doer A horse that thrives on whatever feeding is available; an unfussy feeder.

Hocks well engaged A horse with this feature strides well with the hind legs with a good muscular action and a good bend of the hock joints. The hind legs are well 'under' the horse,

not trailing, with the hind feet stepping at least into the print of the forefeet, or *tracking up.*

Hocks well let-down A good conformation feature comprising a good length and angle from the point of the hip to the hock, a relatively long second thigh and a relatively short cannon.

On the leg Describes a horse that appears to have too little body for its length of leg, or, conversely, a horse with legs that appear too long for its body.

Pace A gait in which the horse at trot moves the legs on each side of the body together in pairs, instead of diagonally. Also known as *ambling.*

Quarters The hind part of the horse. Because the horse impels itself forward from the quarters, *good quarters* are those that are strong and muscular.

Shoulder For a riding horse, a *good shoulder* is one with a considerable slope from the withers to the breast; this gives the horse a pleasing and comfortable stride. A *straight shoulder* is more upright; it shortens the stride and is not so comfortable, but is acceptable for a harness horse.

Sickle hocks Hocks that are curved like a sickle when seen from the side — a poor conformation feature.

Straight action The motion of the horse in which the forelegs move straight and true from the shoulder, with no swinging out of line of the feet. The hind legs follow in alignment.

Substance Describes a horse that is well-made, with good bone, and capable of carrying a fair weight for its size.

Up to weight Capable of carrying a heavy rider.

Well modelled Refers particularly to the head. A well-modelled head has a bone structure that is clearly visible, with the cheek curving up to a well-defined, not thick or fleshy, throat.

Index

Note: page numbers printed below in *italics* refer to illustrations

ACKNOWLEDGEMENTS

The author and publishers wish to thank the following for their help in supplying photographs
for this book on the pages indicated:

All-Sport Photographic Ltd 8 (left, Peter Greenland), 31 (top right), 75 (top, Don Morley);
Animal Photography Ltd 8 (right), 10 (top right, bottom left, bottom right), 11 (top left, bottom
left), 13, 14, 16–17, 31 (top left, bottom), 32, 33, 34, 36, 37, 42, 43, 46, 47, 49 (top), 50,
54, 58–59, 60, 61, 62 (top, bottom left), 65, 70, 71, 72, 73, 75 (bottom), 76, 77, 78 (left), 80,
81, 82 (left), 84, 85, 86, 87, 88–89, 90, 91 (top), 93, 94, 95, 96, 97, 98, 99, 100, 101, 102, 103,
104, 105, 108, 110 (left), 112, 116 (left), 117, 118–19, 120; *Australian News and Information
Bureau* 107 (bottom); *British Museum* 22 (bottom), 25 (top, Michael Holford); *British Tourist
Authority* 27 (bottom); *Peter Clayton* 21 (bottom); *Bruce Coleman* 11 (top right, Eric
Crichton), 20 (right, Jane Burton), 29 (top left, Eric Crichton; top right, Charles Henneghien),
35 (Hans Reinhard), 45 (Eric Crichton), 51 (Jane Burton); *Colour Library International* 16
(top); *Daily Telegraph* 39 (Patrick Ward); *Mary Evans Picture Library* 23, 24 (bottom), 25
(bottom); *Sonia Halliday* 21 (top); *George G. Harrap & Co Ltd* 111 (Sally Ann Thompson);
Michael Holford 20 (left); *Kit Houghton* 4–5, 41, 74, 113, 115, 121, 122 (bottom); *Alan
Hutchison* 27 (top); *Irish Horse Board* 44; *Jacana* 6–7; *Keystone* 122 (top); *Leslie Lane* 11
(centre), 29 (bottom), 40, 48–49, 52, 53, 54–55 (top), 55, 56, 57, 114, 119 (top); *Mansell
Collection* 22 (top), 26 (D. Robinson); *NHPA* 11 (bottom right, J. B. Free), 107 (bottom, Douglas
Dickins); *Picturepoint* 27 (top), 116 (right); *Radio Times Hulton Picture Library* 106; *Roebild*
79; *Jacques Six* 10 (top left), 63 (bottom), 64, 66, 67; *Spectrum Colour Library* 83 (A.
Stainton), 109; *ZEFA* 24 (top V. Wentzel), 38 (J. Behnke), 68–69 (E. Bordis), 91 (bottom,
Revers-Widauer), 92 (Revers-Widauer).
Picture Research: Penny Warn.